POLICEWOMAN ONE

DISCARD

POLICEWOMAN ONE

MY TWENTY YEARS ON THE LAPD

GAYLEEN HAYS
with KATHLEEN MOLONEY

VILLARD BOOKS

NEW YORK 1992

Library of Congress Cataloging-in-Publication Data

Hays, Gayleen.
Policewoman one: my twenty years on the LAPD / by Gayleen Hays
with Kathleen Moloney.
p.   cm.
ISBN 0-394-58528-3
1. Hays, Gayleen.   2. Police—California—Los Angeles—Biography.
3. Policewomen—California—Los Angeles—Biography.   4. Los
Angeles
(Calif.) Police Dept.—Biography.   I. Moloney, Kathleen.
II. Title.   III. Title: Policewoman number one.
HV7911.H39A3   1992
363.2'092—dc20   90-50674
[B]

9 8 7 6 5 4 3 2
First Edition

I hope this book will rest peacefully next to the Ledger, a diary of stories and poetry written by my mothers before me, and passed from mother to daughter.

ACKNOWLEDGMENTS

This book started with a phone call from a friend, Michael Formica. He was producing a movie about a cop, and he needed a technical adviser. It was while I was on the set of that movie that I decided to write *Policewoman One*. Another friend, Calvin Clements, Jr., introduced me to an agent, Jack Dytman of ICM, here in Los Angeles. Jack arranged for me to meet Esther Newberg, his colleague at ICM in New York, and Peter Gethers of Villard Books. They suggested asking Kathleen Moloney to help me write the book, and her agent, Dominick Abel, joined the group, along with Diane Reverand, publisher of Villard. Soon thereafter a book was born, for which I thank them all.

For twenty years I worked with a great group of intelligent, resourceful women, who helped me, taught me, and made me laugh. I am especially grateful to Captain Connie Speck, Sergeant Nan Allomong, Sergeant Midge Watkins, Detective Carole Coan, Detective Karol Chouinard, Detective Sherry Santor, Detective Sandy Hendricks, Detective Charlene Remming, Detective Karen Fleming, Detective Connie Davies, Detective Pat Fogerson, Detective Barbara Arnold, Detective Kay Gates, Detective Sandy Palmer, Sergeant Fanchon Blake, Sergeant Marie Little, Sergeant Joan Simpson, Sergeant Chloe Gilmore, Policewoman Pattie Scroggs, Policewoman Betsy Gray, Officers Sharon Fried, Irene Frizzell, Iris Marshal, and Karen Fleming, and Station Officer Glenda Lombardo. If I had a role model, it would have to be Policewoman Caroyl Hollister, who ran the Van Nuys Jail with style and compassion. I also want to thank my Police Academy classmates: Sharmella Garrett, Rita Knecht, Shilah Johnson, Pat Berry Russell, Angelea Morris, Ces Dominguez, Bobbie Minor, Gail Ryan, and Charlene Daniels. Together we made up the Mighty Ten.

And now for the roll call of the men in my career, the great guys who taunted, inspired, beguiled, or attempted to supervise me: Chief Tom Reddin, Chief Ed Davis, Chief Daryl Gates, Deputy Chief Jesse Brewer, Deputy Chief Dan Sullivan, Commander Joseph Gunn, Captain Carlos Cudio, Lieutenant Richard Pooler, Lieutenant Ron Seban, Lieutenant Don Kitchen, Sergeant Bruce Blake, Sergeant John

ACKNOWLEDGMENTS

. . . . .

Rye, Sergeant George Barber, Sergeant Ed Brayten, Sergeant Fred Haptonstal, Sergeant Ray Paleszewski, Sergeant Gail Tam, Sergeant Ted Hansen, Sergeant Bob Caples, Sergeant Paul Matson, Sergeant Joe Morgan, Sergeant Douglas Reid, Detective Richard Hill, Detective Russel Young, Officer Victor Farhood, Sr., Officer Dave Buck, Officer Danny Staggs, Officer Larry Spencer, Officer Lester Edgedy, Officer Lou Sleger, and Judge Michael Hoff. Special thanks go to Captain Earl Sansing, who knows where all the bodies are buried, and to my favorite sergeant, Allan Dunn, my second husband, and his two daughters, Teri and Donna, my lifetime love children.

Thanks go, too, to my teachers, Al Russio, Lev Mailer, and Joan Jones, for showing me how to draw from the scrapbook of my emotions and transfer them to paper.

And loving thanks to Gay Dawn Tamplin—Everybody's Girl to the world but Mommy to me—and to my sister, Laurel. My final, and my greatest, thanks go to my husband, Mark, and my magical daughter, Serina, for all their love and support.

CONTENTS

PROLOGUE

I was still on probation—I had graduated from the Academy, and the LAPD was still deciding whether or not I was in fact going to be a cop—when I got the word from Vice. I'd been working Juvenile for about a month, but I'd been picked to "operate" a pimp who was suspected of working out of an apartment in "Hollyweird."

For the assignment, I wore a strapless dress. While I was getting briefed, the guys at Van Nuys Division taped my wire on. I could feel the sweat on my body drip down around the tape and slowly trickle down my stomach. It itched like crazy.

By the time I found the place where I was supposed to hook up with my new partner, Carl, I was dazed with fear. I wasn't afraid of getting hurt. I was afraid that if I screwed up this assignment, I'd be history as far as undercover work was concerned. I had to show I could cut it, and this was my one shot. The LAPD was like a small town; there were no secrets. If I wanted to establish myself as an operator, I'd have to score the first time.

"You look perfect, kid," Carl told me. "You'll do fine." Then he grinned, just slightly. "Don't worry. You're *supposed* to look scared."

Carl then gave me my final briefing. He'd be outside with the rest of the team. As soon as I gave them the password—which they'd hear courtesy of my wire—they'd be inside the pimp's apartment in a flash to save the day (and my ass). I took a deep breath—a very deep breath—and headed toward the side door he'd pointed out to me.

"One last time," he said. "What's the password?"

"Mother," I answered. It was my choice. I'd decided I could fit that word into any conversation, even one with a pimp. I figured it might even bring me luck.

As soon as I entered the pimp's room, I knew it wasn't going to be easy. My mind kept racing over the elements of arrest, but my nose told me to get the hell out of there. This asshole looked mean, *real* mean. I faked a smile, but all he did was stare back. He didn't say a word. As I started to lower myself down onto a filthy overstuffed couch across from where he sat behind a desk, I noticed a shotgun leaning upright in the corner behind him. Following my eyes with his, he finally spoke.

"You don't need to worry about that," he said. "That's just my insurance."

"I'm not worried," I told him, one of the biggest lies I'd ever told in my life. I then proceeded to tell him the cover story I had rehearsed. I needed to hook because my boyfriend had suddenly dumped me. I had no friends or family. I needed money desperately. I was broke. As I rambled on, I tried to think how to get that shotgun out of his range before Carl and the guys burst through the door. I was amazed at how easily the bullshit poured out of my mouth as my mind worked like crazy to keep track of the info he was feeding back to me—the details of how it was going to work if he decided to become my pimp.

He started explaining how much I could expect for head jobs, straight sex, butt fucks, and he patiently went over some terms I might be unfamiliar with but which I'd better *get* familiar with, such as "golden shower."

As he talked, I casually moved from the edge of the couch and sat on the edge of his desk. Finished with his lecture, he started to unzip his pants. It took one of my better acting jobs to hide my shock when he reached for his cock and said, "Okay, honey, now let's see how much I can teach you before I send you out on your own."

I smiled sexily, crossed over in front of him, and said, "I don't think my *mother* would approve of what I'm going to do."

"You don't have to think about your mother, honey," he told me. "*I'm* your mother now."

I leaned over his head, reaching for the shotgun. "You might be my mother, but that thing scares me. Why don't I move . . ."

I suddenly jumped behind him, knocking over the floor lamp, and grabbed for the shotgun with one hand. The pimp grabbed with me, and it became a battle of strength. It was like a bizarre tug of war, both of us pulling to gain control of the lethal weapon. And then the tug of war was over as Carl kicked in the door and cops flew into the room. There was a stunned silence as they took in the scene: the pimp with one hand on my arm, the other on his zipper, trying to close it up. When the pimp was safely cuffed, Carl choked back a snicker and said, "Well, it looks like our girl caught her first motherfucker."

That night I was so overwhelmed with excitement, I couldn't sleep. I'd pulled it off. I'd done it. All my life I had searched for something I could do well. I had never found that one thing I could point to and say, "I'm good at that." Everything I'd tried bored me before I could master it. I was one of those children who was always starting *something*—starting dancing, starting cooking, starting to play the violin, even starting scuba diving. But I never finished. If I hadn't become a cop, I probably would have been a drifter, always sampling different life-styles, never settling down.

I'd spent my life looking for a family, for a home. I was searching for something that would give me a feeling of doing someone some good. Now, here I was, a cop. And as a cop I could protect—and feel protected. I could give— and get back even more than I was giving.

That night, thinking of my first "motherfucker," I knew my search was over. I was finally home.

POLICEWOMAN ONE

POLICEWOMAN ONE

The motto "To Protect and to Serve" states the essential purpose of the Los Angeles Police Department. The Department protects the right of all persons within its jurisdiction to be free from criminal attack, to be secure in their possessions, and to live in peace. The Department serves the people of Los Angeles by performing the law enforcement function in a professional manner, and it is to these people that the Department is ultimately responsible.

—FROM THE 1989 LAPD FIELD MANUAL
(RULE 110)

In October of 1989, when I retired from the Los Angeles Police Department after putting in my twenty years, the LAPD retired my number. POLICEWOMAN #1 is what it says on my badge. Once I left the force, there would be no such thing as a uniformed policewoman in these parts anymore—the times and the lingo had changed. Now I know how Willie Mays and Sandy Koufax must have felt, not to mention the *Tyrannosaurus rex*. My species was about to become extinct.

I've always looked forward to retirement parties. With their mixed-up schedules cops don't get a lot of chances to get together and enjoy one another. Once a year or so we're summoned for Training Day, and then, of course, there are the funerals, but it's really only at retirement parties that we get a chance to relax and swap stories. That's the thing about cops. We *love* to talk shop. It's not just fun, it's pretty damn useful to get a lead on the unofficial information that's floating through the grapevine. I also have to admit, those parties let me satisfy a great curiosity—seeing what cops choose to wear when they're out of uniform.

There was a decent turnout for my retirement party, and a bunch of us sat around for hours trading stories about the good old days. Eventually we got to my roasting, and one of my old partners, Karol Chouinard, brought up that fateful day over in West Valley Division when "Gayleen lowered the flag."

The flag in question was a monstrous thing. If I were still in uniform, I'd probably say it was a real motherfucker. It hung out like an old bleached sheet in front of the West Valley station on Vanowen Boulevard in beautiful downtown Reseda. Every day some poor sucker had to raise that flag in the morning and take it down in the evening. No one was crazy about the assignment, especially when the weather was less than balmy. On this particular evening the wind was howling, and it was just starting to rain. The lucky soul assigned to flag duty had called in sick, which led to a major discussion about who was going to take his place.

I'm still not sure how it happened, but somehow I was elected. That must have been the night chivalry officially kicked the bucket; I was the only woman working in West Valley back then, and none of the guys had the *huevos* to brave the elements. I was wearing my official policewoman's uniform—straight skirt, blue shirt and tie, and high heels— plus a red wig. All in all, the perfect ensemble for taking down a flag in gale-force winds.

My buddies stayed warm and dry behind the safety of their desks while I slunk out into the rain to do my duty. Some of the guys watched from the window, suspecting that they were in for a show. I didn't disappoint them. The wind was blowing like mad, whipping my wig into my eyes, and within a few minutes my skirt and blouse were plastered to my body by the rain. I looked more like the winner of a sleazy wet T-shirt contest than a respectable police officer. I undid the rope and started lowering the flag, but I could hardly see what I was doing. If you look in the dictionary under the word "shambles" you'll get a picture of me struggling in the rain that night. I don't get embarrassed easily, but I sure as hell felt self-conscious out there. Even people just driving by were stopping to stare. When I glanced back at the station, I could see that *all* the guys were watching now. Most of them were laughing, too.

That's when I caught my heel on the rope. One minute I was standing upright, flag in hand. The next minute I was doing a pretty fair imitation of a flamingo, with one foot on the ground and the other high in the air. Then, to make matters even worse, the rope snaked between my legs and started pulling my skirt up. When I tried to disengage myself—very casually, of course—I caught my other foot in the rope. The next thing I knew I was totally off balance. Before I could catch myself, I landed flat on my tailbone, right on top of the United States flag and in front of the entire West Valley station. To add insult to injury, my wig flew off and landed in the middle of a puddle.

I hurt like hell, but crying on duty was not an option. So I decided to laugh. Certainly that's what the guys in the station were doing—everyone, that is, except the captain. When he heard the ruckus and saw what had happened, he ran out of the station like a bat out of hell to tell me exactly what he thought of my unprofessional behavior. It wasn't too hard to tell he was not at all happy at the sight of one of his police officers lying on Old Glory with her skirt up around her waist.

"Officer Dunn [Dunn was the name of my husband at the time], would you please get up and explain what in the *fuck* is going on?" he said.

I noticed that he was standing on my wig. I also saw that several of my colleagues had come outside to listen in. One of them was kind enough to put my wig back on my head— backward—when the captain momentarily looked away.

"I'd like to, Captain," I answered, "but unfortunately I can't move."

It was true. I was still caught in the rope, and all I could do was lie there and wait for somebody to set me free.

The captain's eyes widened. Clearly he was even more upset than on the Halloween night I wore my monkey mask for inspection. He couldn't even speak for a minute. Then he said, in a roar that even the guys back inside the station could hear, *"Gayleen, can't you ever fly with the flock?"*

I didn't respond. I figured his question was rhetorical anyway. Captain Higgs knew better than anyone that if I'd answered him, I would have had to say no. I've never even *wanted* to fly with the flock. I don't think I could do it even if I tried. Ever since I was a little girl, I've always been out of synch with the rest of the crowd. (What do you expect from the granddaughter of a madam and the daughter of a burlesque dancer?) That's one of the reasons I became a policewoman in the first place.

One of the last things I did before I left the force was to take a look at all the Performance Evaluation Reports—we called them Rating Reports—that I'd gotten over the years. Once every six months every cop on the force is evaluated by his or her immediate supervisor, and the comments, favorable and unfavorable, are all put down in black and white—like school report cards except that we didn't have to get our parents to sign them. We signed them ourselves. Mine were reasonably positive overall, but I couldn't help noticing a few recurring themes scattered throughout the pages: "Gets easily sidetracked," "Becomes too involved with victims," and "Sometimes loses professional objectivity" showed up a few times. "Seems to be accident-prone" appeared soon after my encounter with the West Valley flag. And then there was my favorite one of all, signed by John Rye, one of my favorite sergeants: "Officer is the last holdout in the uniformed Policewoman position." Truer words were never spoken.

✳ In 1967, when I first joined the LAPD, there were two separate categories on the force: policemen and policewomen. The setup was simple and straightforward. The men wore pants and worked in the field; the women wore skirts and stayed in specialized areas: working the jail, handling the Juvenile division, or doing desk work. Women weren't assigned regular patrol (except the J car, where juveniles were involved) or traffic.✳They couldn't rise above the rank of sergeant or work Burglary, Homicide, or Metro Motors. Policewomen were totally separate from the men on the force.✳

Then, in 1972, everything changed. Claiming discrimination, women, in particular a woman named Fanchon Blake, demanded equal treatment on the force—better assignments, equal status, and the same opportunities for advancement as the men—and, after much fighting and a big lawsuit, they got it. Even after the legal ruling, many of the authorities didn't go along with the policewomen's demands. After the powers that be—all men—were forced to reconsider their discriminatory practices and change their ways, Chief Ed Davis's "concession" speech went something like this: "All right, ladies. You want to be treated like men, you'll dress like men, and you'll go through the Academy like men."

✳ Then the other shoe dropped. In order to achieve equal status, it was explained to us, all policewomen would have to go back through the Police Academy for a few weeks of extra physical and patrol training—becoming "field certified" it was called—and they would have to trade in their skirts and high heels for a pair of men's pants and a pair of men's shoes. That was the price of equality. From that day forward there would be no such thing as a policewoman. Everyone would be a "police officer."

Everyone, that is, except me. I, of course, decided I didn't want to fly with the flock.

It's not that I didn't appreciate the great victory that had been achieved by the women on the force. I did. I knew as well as anyone that there was no reason to keep female police officers out of patrol cars and off the streets. There was no reason women couldn't work Homicide or become lieutenants as well as men. It's just that I had been a police-woman for five wonderful years by then, and I loved my job just the way it was. I felt—and still feel—that the image of a policewoman was different from that of a policeman. There were times it was important for me to project the fact that I was indeed a woman. I needed the flexibility. I don't think there can be a unisex approach to police work. I've been in too many situations—some quite dangerous—where it's better to have a nurturing female persona than that of a confrontational male. On the other hand, there's nothing better than a man when it's time to kick ass. So when it was my turn to make the switch, I told them, politely but firmly, no. I was fine just as I was, thank you very much.

One by one, every other woman on the force made the transition from policewoman to police officer, going through the Academy again, trading in their skirts for trou-sers and the possibility of higher rank. The majority of them never actually went out into the field; most became detectives or moved into plainclothes staff positions. Of the ten women in my graduating class, I'm the only one who didn't eventually become a detective or a staff officer.

I'm not sure why exactly—maybe they just liked to see all their ducks in a row—the brass kept after me, trying to persuade me to join the others. I didn't have to make the change, they made that clear, but they sure as hell couldn't understand why I didn't want to. Every few months I'd get another call. "Are you *sure* you don't want to get field certified?" they kept asking. "Think about how much better it will be for you if you do." I kept saying thanks for the concern, but no.

What they didn't understand was that I had no problem with the new requirements they had outlined. I had nothing against furthering my education or improving my skills. In fact, I ended up doing practically everything necessary to get field certified, not because I had to but because I wanted to. I took all the classes and learned how to use the baton and the other equipment. But I would *not* give up my badge, and I would *not* give up my skirt. I'd worked my butt off to earn the right to wear both of them, and I was proud of them. No one was going to take either of them away from me without a fight.

That's how I became a dinosaur.

One day I was standing in a roll-call room, getting ready for an inspection, polishing the silver buttons on my shirt pockets, when Deputy Chief Dan Sullivan walked by. I watched his eyes flit over the female officers in their men's uniforms. Then he looked at me.

"Officer Hays," he said.

"Yes, sir," I answered, with my stomach in, head up and chest high.

"You are a dinosaur," he told me, and walked away.

The nickname stuck. The Dinosaur. One of my partners, Lester Edgedy, even gave me a dinosaur pin to wear on my shirt.

The last time I got a call from the chief's office, the woman on the other end of the line gave me one more chance. "Are you *sure*?" she kept asking me. Yes, I answered, I'm absolutely sure. Today, nearly twenty years later, I'm still convinced that I made the right decision. At least for me.

There's no question that becoming a police officer would have had its advantages. I would have made more money as I advanced through the ranks, and that would have given me a broader choice of assignments. The extra money would have come in handy, of course, but getting promoted never held any great appeal for me. ("Not promotion-oriented" is how one of my Rating Reports described me.) From what I've been able to tell, moving up in rank doesn't give a cop more satisfying assignments or a happier life; it just allows him to tell other cops what to do. A sergeant friend of mine told me he advanced in rank just so he'd have one less supervisor to answer to. But bossing other people around is not my idea of a good time. I'd rather keep my options open, working the street. I thrived on the chaos out there on the front lines. I loved going undercover.

If I'd gone on to be a detective, my life would have been a lot less complicated, I suppose. In addition to the better pay I could have worked the day shift all the time, and I would have had weekends off to spend with my husband and daughter. I would have had all the holidays off and a lot more prestige. (People are a lot more impressed if you say you're a sergeant or a detective than if you identify yourself as a cop, but I never gave a *shit* about prestige. The department is chock full of asslickers already. Ask any street cop.) I also would have been up to my ears in paperwork much of the time, and I would have spent half a lifetime wading through all the boring and meticulous follow-up—like testifying in court—that is intrinsic to the life of a detective.

What I *like* is helping victims and putting bad guys in jail, and for twenty years as a "lowly" policewoman that's exactly what I did. Officially I was assigned to Patrol most of the time, but I ended up being loaned out to nearly every interesting detail in the city. I rarely felt limited or inhibited by my badge. If there was an assignment I wanted, whether I was officially "certified" to perform the job or not, I usually found a way to get it. I was always looking for a crack in the system.

I didn't always do things by the book—and neither, thank God, did the people responsible for giving me my assignments—but I always found a way to follow the action. Sure, I growled when I got called in the middle of the night to work an emergency twelve-hour shift—but I was secretly thrilled to be right in the middle of the excitement. That's what kept me going. I worked hookers and pimps for Vice. I finagled an assignment to Homicide. I even spent a month on COBRA, a specialized undercover unit focused on catching hard-core, incorrigible, and very dangerous criminals. I've gone undercover to expose gambling rings and to track down rapists, and I've helped hundreds of abused kids. And I did it all with my Policewoman badge.

If that makes me a dinosaur, so be it. Believe me, life may be tougher when you don't fly with the flock, but it's a lot more interesting.

MISS FUZZ

The Los Angeles Police Department expects a very high level of professional conduct from all employees; however, members of the department frequently perform their duties in a manner exceeding the highest standards of the department.

—FROM THE 1989 LAPD FIELD MANUAL
(RULE 220.15)

There were a lot of unusual things about my twenty-year career in the Los Angeles Police Department, but I'd have to say that the most unusual of them all was being voted Miss Fuzz. Most police officers who end up on the front page of newspapers or on national TV get there because they perform some incredible feat of heroism or maybe some shameful and dastardly deed. The first time I made headlines it was because of how I looked in hot pants.

Today, almost twenty years later, I'm still hearing about that police department beauty contest. Hardly a week goes

by that someone doesn't say, "Hey, weren't you Miss Fuzz?"
or "Didn't I see you on Johnny Carson?" When my retirement was written up in the paper, the headline said, LA'S
LAST POLICEWOMAN RETIRES, but there was a juicy para-
graph devoted to my tenure as Miss Fuzz. If *The New York
Times* publishes my obituary when I die, I fully expect it to
say something like, GAYLEEN HAYS DIES AT 102. WAS MISS
FUZZ 1972.

The "Miss Fuzz" episode of my career provided a lot of
laughs for a lot of people, but the person who got the biggest
kick out of the whole thing was my mother. She just
couldn't stop laughing at my title. You see, back in the
mid-fifties, when my mother was a headliner on the burlesque circuit, billed as "Gay Dawn, Everybody's Girl,"
comedians were specifically forbidden to use the word
"fuzz." The code of conduct was amazingly strict in the
fifties. Every town had a different set of rules, usually set
down by the police commissioner or the vice squad, and it
was tricky for the strippers to keep them all straight.

I got very good at knowing the rules myself, since I spent
a significant part of my childhood backstage at one nightclub or another, helping my mother with her costumes,
keeping an eye out for the police, and trying to be inconspic-
uous. Just about every town had a "Don't work the floor"
rule, which meant that the strippers weren't permitted to
get down on the floor and move suggestively. Once in a
while someone would try to get away with lowering herself
to the floor and pretending to have sex, but the authorities
who hadn't been bribed would step in and put a stop to it.

Strippers weren't allowed to work the curtains either, and that really cramped their style. There's nothing more sensuous than the creative use of curtains in a strip act, and all the girls knew it. Even I knew the value of a curtain as a prop. When I was eight years old and determined to create a show-stopping strip act of my own, playing with the curtain while wearing second-hand costumes—presents from some of the girls—before the theater opened was my favorite pastime. I also developed a pretty decent technique for bumping and grinding. I wanted to grow up to be just like Mom.

Some cities were a lot stricter than others. Everybody agreed that Boston was the worst. In Boston, the strippers used to have to wear four pairs of panties. What's even worse, there was always sure to be some creepy-looking public servant who would pay the girls a visit backstage to count the panties—in private, of course. In Boston, and in just about every other city, showing any pubic hair was strictly forbidden, so all the dancers eventually shaved theirs off to keep from accidentally getting into trouble. However, every once in a while some sleazy place would ignore the rules and try to intimidate strippers into showing their pubic hair. In fact, in those places the audience would expect it and would stomp and yell and create a huge ruckus if they didn't get to see any.

That's how my mother came to invent what she called her Stripper's Pubic Wig. One night after listening to a frustrated audience calling out for a little more than what they were getting, she came home from the drugstore with a large piece of moleskin, a wire brush, and a jar of glue. Completely mesmerized, I sat on the edge of her bed and watched her work. First she trimmed the bristles off the brush. Then she glued them, one by one, to the piece of moleskin, and sprinkled face powder over the whole thing to give it a "flesh tone." When her handiwork was complete, she divided the moleskin into several pieces, one for each of the girls in the show. With the help of a little more glue and a little more makeup, all the strippers had instant pubic hair. From that night on, the customers got their money's worth.

No matter which town a club was in, rules were toughest on the feature acts—which my mother always was—because they went on late in the show. By that time two things were certain: the audience would be rowdy, and the cops were sure to be there. Strippers who came on early might get away with some raunchy stuff, but as a feature, my mother used to have to get by on her talent, beauty, and ingenuity. Her act had to be clean enough to win the cops' seal of approval but provocative enough to keep the customers on the edge of their seats. No one could match my mother at walking that fine line between healthy sexuality and raunch. (She got her stage name "Everybody's Girl" because she had the look of the girl next door, or at least the girl everybody *wished* lived next door.) She was never arrested, and she was never out of work. She developed a reputation as a "troubleshooter" stripper, someone who could go out on stage and take care of a rowdy crowd.

Now that I have a young daughter of my own, I find it

nearly impossible to believe that I was really there to be a part of all that. I wish there had been videos back then, so that Serina could know what her grandmother was like and how she could drive men wild with just a look. I'm sorry that my daughter never had the weird but wonderful experience of the burlesque circuit. When I was growing up in and around nightclubs, I *loved* it—all of it. I was proud of my mother, and I thought she was beautiful. (She still is. She has one of those ageless faces, and her body is in better shape than those of most thirty-year-olds.) I never go anywhere without my favorite picture of her. There she is, Gay Dawn, Everybody's Girl, at her peak, looking gorgeous as she poses behind her barely-big-enough sombrero.

I suppose that another of the reasons I enjoyed the life was that my mother was a star. As one of the top acts at the time, right up there with Lili St. Cyr and Tempest Storm, she played big clubhouses and opened up all of the top shows, including the Magic Castle and the Body Shop. Sure, I knew that she wasn't exactly your average chocolate-chip-cookie-baking mom, but life was never dull when she was around and I loved and worshiped her. I thrived on the eccentric people she surrounded herself with, the odd schedule she kept, and the fantasy life she inspired in me. I adored going to school in furs that were "left over" from the nightclubs' checkrooms or showing up at dances in Mommy's stripper dresses and jewelry.

As strange as it seems, I believe that what I learned then has given me my healthy attitude about sex. Being raised with burlesque dancers has made me comfortable around people who are up-front about their sexuality and not afraid to show their feelings. I've always enjoyed people who are attractive and sensual—and who *know* they're attractive and sensual. There's nothing quite like the confidence of a good stripper, an attitude that says, "Aren't I gorgeous when I take my clothes off? Aren't we all enjoying this?" Back then I used to feel sorry for the women who weren't good-looking enough to be up there and lucky enough to be in show business.

My mother was forty-seven years old the year she hung up her G-string and retired, exactly the same age I was when I stopped being a cop. I still have vivid memories of the many clubs she played and the charismatic people we met along the way. I put together a scrapbook of all my mother's clippings, and I stashed the posters and other paraphernalia in an old trunk of my grandmother's. I've kept it all, every trinket, picture, and costume. When I comb through the memorabilia today, I can almost smell the cigar smoke, see the pasties and the feathers, and hear my mother running through the list of rules, including her own favorite: "Gay-leen," she used to say to me at least once a week, "always leave something to the imagination."

I kept her advice very much in mind when I tried out for Miss Fuzz.

IN CASE YOU haven't noticed, let me be the first to tell you: Los Angeles is a show business town. No one in L.A. is immune to the power and the attraction of the movie business, not even the Los Angeles Police Department. When someone uses the word "killer," there's a good chance he's describing a hot new movie or anything other than a murderer.

In June of 1972 I was working the night shift in the Van Nuys jail when I got a phone call from a policewoman who was working downtown in Public Affairs. I'm not sure why she called *me,* but I can remember very vividly what she proposed. In order to generate publicity for a new movie called *Fuzz*—a part-comedy, part-drama starring Burt Reynolds as a cop, Yul Brynner as the bad guy, and Raquel Welch as the policewoman with *oomph*—the movie company wanted to sponsor a police department beauty contest. All interested women in the department were encouraged to participate, and the winner would be named "Miss Fuzz." According to the woman from Public Affairs, it was going to be a piece of cake. It would be helpful for the department's image, she explained, because it would show the world that policewomen are really *feminine.* Think how much it will help with recruitment, she said. In short, she did a major selling job, which worked on me and about twenty other women on the force.

I realize that the idea of a police department beauty contest would be unthinkable today in the relatively enlightened nineties, even in Los Angeles. (To begin with, it would have to be *Ms.* Fuzz.) But back then it sounded to me and a lot of other people like a real lark. I was always eager for an adventure, and the Miss Fuzz contest sounded like one of the best to come along in a while. I also thought it was a great way to share some laughs with my friends. And besides, I couldn't wait to tell my mother that at last it was all right to say the word "fuzz."

In 1972 *The Feminine Mystique* had already been out for nine years or so, and women's liberation was in full flower out in the real world, but there's no question that the police department was dragging its feet when it came to full-fledged feminism. Yes, there were women on the job, but they were definitely considered a breed apart, so much so that until 1972 we used to have the Los Angeles Policewomen's Fashion Show every year. The models were all policewomen, and husbands and boyfriends were invited to watch. The chief of police always made a point of showing up, along with the deputy chief, the lieutenants, and the rest of the brass. We held it in the auditorium of the Police Academy, with an open bar, a fancy caterer—the works. Officially it was a fund-raiser for a children's charity, but I think we all looked at it as a chance to get together in civilian clothes, gossip, and celebrate being women for a little while. Today we'd call what we did then "networking," I suppose. We talked about good assignments, lousy supervisors, and partners to avoid at all costs. In those days there weren't that many opportunities for women in the department to get together en masse, so I thought that the fashion shows were great. With a total of only about a hundred women on the force, even something as trivial as a fashion show kept us from feeling too cut off. It was nice to feel connected to a colleague, even if it meant acting like a "girl."

When I describe those fashion shows to women on the job today, they look at me as if I'm crazy, but then it all seemed like the most natural thing in the world. Just like the Miss Fuzz contest. The day of the contest about twenty police-women showed up to compete, everyone in hot pants and go-go boots. Unlike the Miss America pageant, the Miss Fuzz contest didn't have a "talent" competition, and there was no one asking us questions to determine whether we were smart or had a good personality (however, I think they should have had a marksmanship competition). All we did was march slowly around a swimming pool and let the judges take a good look at us. Their decision would be final. I no longer remember who did the judging, but I do recall that Ed McMahon did the honors as master of ceremonies.

There were a lot of great-looking women in the contest that day, but I picked Karen Fleming to win. With her athletic body, long legs, and Swedish country-girl face I didn't see how she could lose. What I didn't know—and I don't think anyone else did either, with a few notable excep-tions—was that the outcome of the contest was supposed to have been prearranged. I found out later that the people running the contest had told one of the coordinators that if she would get the contest organized, they would guarantee that she would be the winner. But when the moment of truth arrived, the judges balked and chose me instead of her. (In the photographs it's easy to pick out the woman who had been told the fix was in. She's the one whose mouth is open and who's staring at me in disbelief, as if to say, "*You're* not supposed to win, *I'm* supposed to win.") I was declared Miss Fuzz and given custody of one of the biggest trophies I've ever seen, a woman in a police uniform. The inscription: MOST BEAUTIFUL POLICEWOMAN, MISS FUZZ.

I thought the whole thing was great, and I thoroughly enjoyed both the contest itself and the publicity that followed my victory. Unfortunately my mother couldn't be there for the judging, but I couldn't help thinking about her the whole time I strutted my stuff around the swimming pool. "Leave something to the imagination," I could hear her telling me. Little did I know that the fun was just beginning. The moment the contest was over I was surrounded by newspaper reporters and photographers. There were television cameras there as well, and everyone was sticking a microphone in my face at once. Obviously the makers of *Fuzz* had done their bit to generate publicity for the event, and it was paying off.

Ed McMahon came up to me after the contest and said, "You know, I think you'd be good on Johnny Carson. He'd really enjoy talking to you." On the spot he set up an interview with *The Tonight Show*'s talent screener, and within days I was scheduled as a guest. It was official. Miss Fuzz was about to become a star, for at least five whole minutes.

When the department got wind of the fact that I was going to be making an appearance on *The Tonight Show*, they got nervous, to say the least. In their view, a loose cannon was about to roll off the deck. Two Internal Affairs guys came to see me and pass along some advice. "Before you go on the Carson show, we want you to realize that you're representing the department. Anything you say can reflect on all of us. We think we should take you through some of the questions and make sure you know how to answer them." Then they started in on what I should wear. My full dress uniform would be nice, they said. It was important for the department that I make a good impression.

I listened politely to everything they said and then answered them, in my quietest, firmest voice: "I'm not going to be programmed by you or anyone else," I said. "If I can't say what I want to say, I'm not going on at all. And I'm *not* wearing my uniform. I'm doing this on my own time. Either I'm going out there on my own, or I'm not going at all." They didn't like my reaction, but they'd created this beastess and they'd have to live with her. They couldn't stop me from appearing in civilian clothes but they *could* have made my life miserable. Luckily, they ultimately decided to ignore me.

For all my bravado, I wanted to skip bail the day of my *Tonight Show* appearance. I'd been interviewed a dozen times already, by reporters from newspapers, magazines, radio, and even a little local TV, but this was the Big Time. Naturally all of my friends had some advice—wear your uniform, don't wear your uniform, sit up straight, be sure not to swear, be yourself, don't say anything rude about the force. In the end I decided to wear a skirt, a silk blouse (the first hundred-percent silk blouse I had ever owned), and my lucky boots. And I decided to be myself. By the time I got to the studio and was squirming in my chair in the green room, I began to wonder if show business was really in my blood. I suddenly longed for the morning jail watch—*any* duty but this one.

Minutes before I was supposed to go out and meet Johnny, I stood backstage fluffing up my hair and giving myself a pep talk—"Keep your head up, tuck your tummy in, be sincere," I mumbled to myself. My mouth was dry, and all of a sudden I had no idea what to do with my hands. When I heard Johnny introduce me—"Here's Miss Fuzz, LAPD," he told several million people—my mind went blank and my limbs froze for a second or two. Then the band started playing "The Stripper," and my fog lifted. As if on automatic pilot, I strutted out on stage and did my best stripper imitation, bumping and grinding just the way Gay Dawn used to do it. I didn't work the floor or touch the curtain, and I kept my clothes on, of course. Still, I think the *Tonight Show* audience got the general idea. I'm not sure how Johnny felt about my pseudo-strip, but the audience went wild. They clapped and hooted as I danced my way over to the chair, right next to Pat Boone, Johnny's other guest. By the time I got there, I was relaxed. I forgot about the gun to my head with fifty million people squeezing the trigger.

Johnny asked me some questions about being Miss Fuzz, and I got even more comfortable. Then, when my guard was completely down, he asked me The Question, the one no cop ever wants to hear. "Have you ever had to use your gun?" he wanted to know. I took a deep breath and said, "Well, yes, but the story is kind of embarrassing. You have to promise you won't tell anybody." My expression was completely deadpan.

Looking conspiratorially out at the audience, Johnny promised: "No, we won't tell a soul." The crowd was really laughing now.

I proceeded to tell the story of how, one night when I was first on the force and still on probation, I was taking a shower and heard a loud noise outside my apartment house. When I turned off the water, I could tell it was someone screaming. "My God, somebody help me! He's killing me!" the voice said. I jumped out of the shower, grabbed my gun, and ran out into the backyard.

At this point I really started to warm to the story. I got out of my chair next to Johnny and began to act it out. When I ran out into the yard, I saw the man who had been screaming and another man coming after him with a knife, obviously trying to stab him. Out of the corner of my eye I saw my neighbor across the way, but my first thought was to stop the guy with the knife. I hollered for him to stop where he was and pointed my gun at him. He stopped, all right, and he stared at me. The victim stared too. So did my neighbor. That's when I realized that I had forgotten to put any clothes on. They were all staring at me, but no one even noticed my gun. All they could see was me, naked.

All of a sudden I could see the next morning's headlines: NAKED POLICEWOMAN SHOOTS SUSPECT. All I could think of was, Now I'll *never* make probation.

"What did you do then?" Johnny asked me when I stopped for breath.

"I held the suspect there and told my neighbor to call the police," I said innocently. The audience screamed with laughter, and we cut to a commercial. When I got back to my chair, Pat Boone told me I'd been great. It was good to hear it. I had no idea of how I'd gone over until then.

I don't think I could ever have imagined the impact of that one appearance on television. I got fan mail from all over the world. I was written up in even more newspapers and magazines, and I became a minor celebrity on local television. Someone even started a Miss Fuzz Fan Club, and I got admiring letters from all over the world. When the movie opened, at the Bruin Theater in Westwood, I made a special appearance. Mayor Sam Yorty showed up to shake hands and have his picture taken with me. He turned out to be sincere and very funny. My fellow cops didn't have much to say to me about my new title, but the public loved it. It isn't every day that a police officer gets that kind of support and good feeling from the civilian population, and I really got a kick out of it.

There were no protests at the time of the Miss Fuzz contest, nobody carrying THIS CONTEST EXPLOITS WOMEN picket signs or accusing the LAPD of blatant sexism, but I realize that I got off easy. Today if I or anyone else put on a pair of hot pants and tried out for Miss Fuzz, the protestors would be hip-deep on the ground. Hell, I'd probably even join them. Even so, I'm not one bit sorry I did it. I had a ball, and I didn't feel exploited for a minute. I thought that I showed that the LAPD had a sense of humor and made people think that lady cops might be human after all.

I'm not sure what all this publicity did for *Fuzz,* the movie that started it all—which bombed at the box office, by the way—or whether it furthered Raquel Welch's career, but I know that, for a time at least, I was a star, and I definitely wasn't one of the guys. The department transferred me from the jail to Community Relations, and I spent a large part of the next couple of years making speeches around town, encouraging young women to choose police work as a career, and furthering the reputation of the men and women in blue. LAPD's loose cannon was now secured on deck and blasting away. Or so they thought.

CHILD ABUSE

*Police officers are frequently required to make deci-
sions affecting human life and liberty in difficult
decisions where there is no opportunity to seek advice and little time for reflection.*

—FROM THE 1989 LAPD FIELD MANUAL
(RULE 140.10)

The case started out as a routine custody battle. At least that's what the detectives who were handling it thought it was. The mother had custody of her two little girls, and the father, who had reasonable visitation privileges, had been bringing them home late on weekends and sometimes keeping them a day or two longer than he was supposed to. Old story, new faces: the mother, fed up with her ex-husband's behavior, decided that he shouldn't be allowed to see the kids at all anymore. Her complaints had been escalating over a period of weeks. This time she was

accusing him of molesting the little girls during their overnight stays.

I was on the desk one Sunday afternoon, and the parents
were at it again. The accusations were flying; she said he was
molesting the kids, and he said she was neglecting them.
They were playing dueling obscenities, and the kids just sat
there, staring straight ahead, not looking at either parent. It
broke my heart to see them and I felt their pain, but I tried
not to get involved. The detective in charge of the case had
other ideas, though. He stopped by my desk and said, "Gayleen, I want you to talk to these kids for a minute. I don't
think there's anything there, but I'd feel better if you
checked it out. This mother has a history of these sex
complaints, but we've never been able to pin anything on
the guy."

The detective was probably right. All he wanted was my
rubber stamp. Most cops develop an instinct for distinguish-
ing the legitimate child abuse complaints from the phony
ones—according to regulations, every complaint has to be
followed up, and for every "real" grievance there are quite
a few bogus ones—and this detective's instincts were very
reliable. He'd asked for my help on these kinds of cases
before, and he respected my judgment. I can't say I was ever
happy to be brought in as a "consultant," but getting directly involved with these poor kids was a lot better than
reading about injured kids in the morning paper.

By the time I was brought into this case, the father had
gone home and the kids were sitting in one of the interrogation rooms with their mother. One girl was ten, and the

other had just turned six. Both were clean and nicely dressed, and their hair was neatly combed. One of them had a bow in her hair. The all-American family. It was hard to imagine that anything could be wrong at home.

I walked into the room, took a long look at all three of them, made a little pleasant conversation with the girls, and then asked the ten-year-old if she'd like to come and see where I worked. The first thing a cop has to do when she's interrogating children is to get them alone—away from their siblings and especially away from their parents. No abused child will ever talk about the abuse in front of her parents. I was going to have to interrogate both of the girls, but I decided that it would be easier on the younger child if the older one went first. From the way they were sitting I could tell that the ten-year-old was very protective of her little sister. Abused children are usually more protective of each other than normal kids. Understandably so.

After giving her a little tour of the station I sat her down at a table in a quiet corner. In dealing with kids, scared or otherwise, you have to get past the fact that you're sitting in a police station, so I'm always looking for calm, non-threatening areas to sit. When we got comfortable, I told her my first name and what my job was. I explained that I had a daughter at home, just about the same age as her little sister, and that I loved my daughter very much. Then I took off my badge and let her hold it while we talked. I was in my uniform, and that can be intimidating to a child too. I always did whatever I could to lighten the atmosphere and make myself appear less formidable. I wanted to be a trustworthy authority figure without being scary. In other words, I let the mother in me do the talking.

When I thought the little girl was as relaxed as she was going to get, I began the interrogation. I started with, "It must be really hard when you have to go back and forth between Mommy and Daddy," and gradually, as I asked more and more questions, she opened up to me. I began to get a picture of her home life. To be honest, I went into the interrogation thinking that there was nothing there, just as the detective had said. After all, he specialized in child abuse cases, and he knew his stuff. Somehow, though, in the middle of my routine questioning, I got an eerie feeling about that little girl. There was a look in her eyes that told me she was afraid, hiding something. Without saying the words, she was asking me to help her, to give her permission to tell the truth.

I stopped asking questions and instead started to talk. Keeping my voice soft and low and moving a little closer to her, I put my arm around her. I knew that my job now was to remove any guilt she might be feeling about her parents and her sister and even herself. I needed to let her know that I understood what she was going through.

"When I was a little girl about your age, a man did something bad to me," I began. "I thought it was my fault. and I never wanted to tell anybody about it. I carried it around inside me for a long time, like a big secret. Then I finally told somebody about it, and I felt a lot better. Don't you think you should talk about what's been happening to you?"

It was working. Her eyes filled with tears, and all of a sudden she began to talk very fast. The story of what her father had been doing to her and her little sister came tumbling out. I didn't even try to take notes as she spilled out her pain. I just hugged her and listened. By the time she stopped for breath, I had learned that the father had definitely been molesting the girls, and for quite a while. When the sisters stayed with their father, they slept in a double bed, and the father used to go in there almost every night, lie in bed with them, and masturbate. "Daddy would rub himself on the sheets" is how the little girl put it.

Sometimes he would fondle the girls, and on a few occasions he tried to penetrate the older girl. Apparently he attempted to get his penis in her vagina, but it wouldn't fit. Lately he had been molesting his younger daughter. As is so often the case, what pushed the ten-year-old over the edge was seeing what her father was doing to her sister. Being the oldest, *she* could take the abuse from her father, but she had to protect her baby sister. She used to lie in bed, pretending to sleep but actually keeping guard over her sister. The girls made a pact never to tell anyone about what was happening, not even their mother.

I didn't bother asking if she ever tried to resist her father, because I already knew the answer. Traumatized, terrified children don't resist; they go limp, the way a bird does when it's being terrorized by a cat. Their hearts beat wildly, but they don't move. They're numb, paralyzed, as if they're under some terrible spell. That's what happened to this little girl.

I'm not sure I can describe what it was like to sit in a tiny corner of the Van Nuys police station and listen to that sweet little girl tell her nightmarish story. I had heard it all before, of course, but that didn't help. It didn't keep me from wanting to cry or scream or kick something, preferably the child's father. I also wanted to spirit her out of the station and take her someplace safe. But I did none of those things, of course. What I did do, though, was give her a secret way of coping, knowing she was going to need it while she waited for our mangled legal system to take some action. "There is a secret place I hide in whenever something scary or bad happens to me. Do you want me to take you there?" I asked.

She nodded.

"Okay, close your eyes and think of a beautiful garden, where you can play with anything you want to, and no one can harm you. If something bad happens to your body you don't like, take yourself to this garden until you're safe again. Do you understand?"

She nodded again, sadly.

I gave her another hug, explained that now I wanted to talk to her little sister, then sent her off for an ice cream in the lunchroom.

Things went much faster with the little girl. She had barely had a chance to look at my badge when she looked up at me and said, "I know what you're gonna ask me, but I don't wanna tell you. We promised."

"I don't blame you," I answered quietly. "I don't want to ask you." I gave her a crayon and said, "Why don't we just color for a while? Let's just color instead." But within seconds she started to sob and told me her version of the story. We had our case. I made my report to the detective, and he took it from there. From then on the children had no unsupervised visits with their father.

I wish I could say that all child abuse cases had such "happy" endings. For every one that works out okay there are many that end tragically. On another Sunday afternoon a woman and a teenage girl came bursting into the station, followed closely by a man who was cursing them and telling them to stop. It didn't take an expert to see that this was clearly not your typical nuclear family.

I can still picture them in my mind. The father was enormous, the mother was medium-sized, and the daughter was very slender and delicate. She was thirteen years old, but she looked ten at the most. It turned out that he had been beating both of them for years. He had been sexually abusing the daughter too, fondling her, sometimes in public, and having sex with her. Most of the time he wouldn't let the girl go to school, and he didn't permit her to have any friends. (Not allowing kids to have friends or go to school is typical of abusive parents.)

In this case the mother filed a complaint, and she got a restraining order to keep him from coming around while she worked on getting a divorce. The problem was, he was such an animal that she couldn't find anyone to serve the restraining order to him. Everyone was too afraid to get near the guy. He used to follow the mother and daughter through the streets all the time, so the mother decided to make his sick, twisted habits work for her. She and her daughter ran straight for the police station, and he followed them all the way.

When she reached the lobby, I was the first police officer she encountered. "I need help," she pleaded. "I have a restraining order to keep my husband away from me, but I need someone to serve it to him." I took one look at the guy and saw why everyone was terrified of him. He looked like King Kong's stunt double. I looked around for some help, but all the guys were conveniently busy. I was the only one available to take on this asshole. I took the restraining order from her, walked up to the guy, handed it to him, and said, "Hey, you've been served. This is it. These are all my witnesses. I've got a whole lobby full of people in here."

I surveyed the crowd and shouted, "Hey, everybody, this guy's been served." I turned back to the monster. "Now get the hell out of here, or I'll throw you in jail."

He stared at the restraining order then turned to his wife with hatred in his eyes. "I'll get even with you, you bitch!" Then, to his daughter, he hollered, "This is all your fault!" He turned away, walked out the door, and fell down the stairs. From where I was standing I could tell the fall was a fake, but he made it look pretty good. His wife knew he was faking too, but the daughter thought he was really hurt. Lying at the bottom of the stairs, he started wailing that his leg was broken and pleading with his daughter to help him.

"This wouldn't have happened if you hadn't started causing trouble," he snarled at her. It was her fault he got hurt, he said, her fault that the family broke up. Everything was her fault. Then he went in for the kill. "Can't you see I can't do anything without you? If you leave me, I'll die."

The daughter never said a word, but I could sense that he was pressing all the right buttons. He wanted her to feel guilty, and she did. A lot of kids who are abused by their fathers have a strange attachment to them, figuring that a lousy father is better than no father at all. It was obvious that he was capable of exerting a tremendous psychological pull over her. Nearly sick to my stomach with disgust from listening to this asshole, I told the guy to get up off the floor and get the hell out of my station. Then I grabbed the daughter by the shoulders and told her, "It's *not* your fault that your father's like this." And I said to the mother, "You have to go someplace he doesn't know. He can't know where you are."

The mother looked hopeless. "I can't afford to move, and I don't have anywhere to go. Besides, I have this restraining order!"

I wanted to scream. Here was a woman whose life was in danger, whose daughter's life was in danger, and she thought that a piece of paper was going to make everything all right.

The three of them left the station, along with the restraining order, and I never saw them again. I read about them, though. A few days later the man went to his wife's house and blew open the front door with a sawed-off shotgun. Then he walked inside, put six shells into his wife, and took his daughter. The last anybody heard of them they were heading south.

▌T WASN'T UNUSUAL for me to be called in to help with a child abuse case. No matter what my official assignment was, abused kids were my specialty and my passion. A few of the detectives knew that I had a way with them, probably because I was a mother myself and something of an amateur psychologist, as most cops are. I'd also developed a track record as a savvy interrogator. What they didn't know—what they couldn't know, because I never talked about it—was that I myself had been abused as a child. I related so strongly to those kids because I used to be one of them. When I held those little girls' hands and told them what had happened to me when I was a little girl, I wasn't acting. It was all true.

I never really knew my father very well. My mother was sixteen when she married him and eighteen when she got pregnant with me. By the time I was born, my father was long gone, along with a lot of the American men in 1942. The difference was, my dad didn't come back after the war was over, at least not very often or for very long. Two weeks after I was born, in Washington, my mother and I moved to an army base in Alabama. My mother did her best to support us but, as a result, from the beginning I was left alone quite a bit. There was always somebody taking care of me, but I had few friends my own age, even after I started going to school. We were always on the move too much for me to make any real attachments.

My childhood memories are somewhat blurry, but I do

remember going from one army base to another all the time. It seemed to me as if we were always on our way somewhere, on a train or a bus, and I was never sure why. I was always waking up in the middle of the night in a dark room and not being able to remember where I was or how to find the bathroom. Maybe that's why I'm still afraid of the dark. Most abused children are.

The molesting started when I was six years old. I was living with my father in a boarding house in Long Beach—one of the few times I lived with him—and my mother used to visit whenever she could get away from work. I was happy at first because there was a woman living right upstairs who had a daughter exactly my age. I was thrilled that they were always inviting me up to have milk and cookies and play games. One of the little girl's favorite games was one she called "Tickle." The two of us would take off our clothes and get into bed. Then she'd touch me all over but especially on my nipples and genitals. And finally she'd put her finger inside me and rub me.

The whole time this was going on, her mother would be watching us. I didn't know what we were doing, and I don't think the other little girl did either. But her mother certainly did. She didn't take her eyes off us for a minute.

I had horribly mixed feelings about those afternoons. On the one hand, I was deliriously happy to have a friend at last. On the other hand, I hated the games. I asked the little girl's mother to tell her to stop. The mother got furious, and she turned on me viciously. She threatened me, saying that if I told my father about "Tickle," she would tell him that it was all my idea. Who did I think my father would believe, an adult or a child? And I could be sure she would find out if I told, because the walls in the boarding house were paper-thin. She could hear everything that was said in any of the rooms. That much was certainly true. No one had any secrets in that flophouse.

The bitch was right. So I was too scared to tell my father or anyone else about the games that were being played upstairs in that apartment. Shortly after that, when my mother was visiting, I begged her and my father to send me to boarding school. Neither of them understood why I was so determined to get away—in fact, I think they were hurt that I didn't want to live with one of them—but they finally agreed to ship me off to the Altadena Boarding School. I have no idea how my mother managed to pay the fees. She was working as an elevator operator in Los Angeles at the time—she didn't go into burlesque until a couple of years later—so she must have lived on franks and beans the whole time I was there.

The next person to molest me was one of the men who worked at the boarding school. First he gave me an enema. When he had finished, he tried to put his penis inside me. But at seven years old my vagina was too small, and it wouldn't fit. During the time I stayed in the boarding school there were many enemas and numerous other encounters.

As a child I was quite striking looking, with long white hair, bright green eyes, and a tall, skinny body. I was always attracting attention, and it was usually the kind I didn't want. "Where did you get that hair?" people would always ask. Or "Come over here and let me take a look at your big green eyes" and "Aren't you a pretty little girl?" I always stood out from the crowd, and I hated that. I used to look at kids who were normal-looking, especially ones who had two parents living at home, and envy them so much I wanted to die.

I was miserable in boarding school. I used to lie awake on the floor at night and wish I were dead. I never slept on my bed if I could help it; every morning in boarding school we had bed inspection. If our beds weren't perfect, we were severely punished. I didn't want to run that risk.

When I got out of boarding school, my mother was performing on the road and couldn't keep me with her, so I went to live with a family who took in other people's kids once in a while. I liked it at first, but after a month or so the lady of the house started beating me. First she'd sit me down and tell me exactly why she was going to punish me and how it was going to hurt her more than it hurt me. Then she'd give me a dose of castor oil, which always made me sick. Finally she would get out a belt buckle or a coat hanger and hit me until she raised welts all over my body.

Once she beat me so badly that somebody turned her in. When the authorities showed up, I lied through my teeth. The cop asked me if the woman had been hurting me, and I looked him right in the eye and said no, I had fallen down the stairs. Once again I had been frightened into covering up the truth. The woman had told me that since my mother didn't want me, if I left her house I was heading back to boarding school.

Unfortunately there would be more beatings and more sexual abuse for me by the time I reached adulthood, but I've never wanted to dwell on it before, and I don't want to belabor it now. The only reason I even mention it is to explain, at least in part, what I believe is my special affinity for abused kids and why I made it my business to become an expert at interrogating them. I've always felt that in helping those kids I've helped myself as well. I think it may also explain why, when I was in college, I was irresistibly drawn to courses in abnormal psychology. I'd always been fascinated by the vagaries of human nature, long before I knew that knowing something about them would help me in my work.

According to department policy, abused girls should always be interviewed by female officers, and little boys should give their statements to a male officer. The thinking here is that girls will be more comfortable talking about being molested to a woman, and boys will feel better if they can speak to a man. That theory sounds good on paper, but frankly I've always thought that policy was a little off, especially the boy-man part. I don't know the exact figures, but a good proportion of the time a boy is molested by a man, so it's not very likely that he'll be completely relaxed when he's asked to open up to a male officer. There's something else wrong with that policy too: there are plenty of male officers who are great with kids of both sexes. I've worked with some who did a much better job than I did.

I love kids, but I'm not entirely comfortable talking to them; I can be very shy around them. I've always wished that I could be one of those people who take to kids right away, who just tune into their wavelength without any effort at all, but I'm not a "natural." I have to work hard to establish a rapport with them. Kids are smart about people, and they sense right away when somebody isn't being straight with them or when people aren't at ease with them.

One of the cardinal rules of police work is that a police officer is not supposed to become personally involved in any case, because if he does, he's likely to lose his professional objectivity. I don't always agree with that rule. First of all, I don't think it's possible for anyone to be objective all of the time. And secondly, I think a little personal involvement can serve as tremendous motivation to get a job done. People used to advise me not to care so much, but I couldn't simply turn off my emotions, especially when I was confronted with abused kids or anyone else who desperately needed my help.

The way I saw it, these people were victims, and when they walked into the police station, I was the only thing standing between them and what they viewed as the end of the world. I always strove to help shatter the myth that police officers are just a bunch of uncaring automatons. I wanted to let victims know that there was a human being on the job, someone who really cared what happened to them. No matter what their problem was, I always tried very hard to calm them down and make them feel comfortable. The police department has plenty of "professionals." I wanted to be a real person. I'm sure I overdid it sometimes, especially with injured children and victims of rape.

Like everything else in police work, the interrogation of a child has to be done by the numbers. The first thing we tried to do during questioning was get the elements of the crime that supposedly has been committed and put it into the correct category—molestation, sexual abuse, rape, sodomy, whatever. Each crime has different elements. If the adult puts his penis inside a child, that's one crime. If he puts his mouth on the child's genitals, it's another. Kissing, breast fondling, taking off clothes, making suggestive remarks—these are just a few elements that define the crime. The city has a whole penal code full of them, and it was my job to get it all down in black and white.

As the interview progressed, I'd make out my report, with elements, names, and dates. I'd write down how old the child was when the incident happened and how many times she was molested. My most important task during the information-gathering process was determining the most important points and recording them concisely. For obvious reasons, kids and other victims of violence often talk incoherently. They're so relieved that someone is listening that they just open the floodgates and let it all out. The interrogator has to allow that to happen and then capsulize the story so that it can be relayed to the appropriate authorities.

When I worked Juvenile, one of the more macabre assignments that I had was to keep the child abuse scrapbook up to date. It was a huge thing, stuffed with names, dates, details, and photographs of child abuse victims. (They kept a scrapbook over in Vice as well, but it was a different kind. Theirs had pictures of pimps and prostitutes to help cops recognize them.) The child abuse scrapbook was horrible in many ways, filled as it was with images of tortured children, but it was also useful. It showed police officers what to look for when they suspected that a child was being hurt.

When a rookie cop was learning the ropes, his training officer didn't have to completely rely on his powers of description. He could simply take out the scrapbook and say, "Check this out, here's what a cigarette burn looks like. Here's what an iron mark looks like. Here's what a broken arm looks like." There were pictures of dead children in the scrapbook as well. In suspected child abuse cases that resulted in death, there was always an autopsy; we wanted to know what other injuries the child had suffered before the one that killed him. The scrapbook was one of our most effective teaching aids. Not many people forgot what they saw there, even if they tried.

Not surprisingly, many police officers become real experts on child abuse after a while. They can just look at a child and know immediately what has been going on behind closed doors, often more accurately than doctors. (And cops are a lot more willing to testify in court than doctors are.) Many times I was asked to go to a crime scene and take pictures of an injured child, and I would go along with the child to the doctor's office to gather more evidence. In child abuse cases—as in all cases—defenders can be very cagey, and unless we were very scrupulous about evidence, we could lose a case on a technicality. In the doctor's office I would have to be careful never to let the child out of my sight, even for a second. If I did, someone was sure to claim that the cuts and bruises in the pictures I took were left by someone else who managed somehow to be in contact with him. I had to be able to go to court and say, "*No*, the doctor did not grab her. *No*, she did not fall down the stairs on the way to the hospital. *Nothing* else happened to that child that would have left a mark."

There are a lot of frustrations in police work—in my twenty years there were plenty of days when I thought the job was one gigantic exercise in futility—but I don't think there's anything more frustrating than child abuse cases. When it comes to dealing with what are now called "dysfunctional families," even success stories can seem like failures. After all, if you've taken kids away from their parents, what have you really accomplished? Sure, you've kept them from being hurt or even killed, but you certainly haven't given them any guarantee of a good life.

Basically, in child abuse cases cops have to destroy a family in order to save a child. When we blow the whistle on someone who is hurting his kids, when we step in and take our pictures and cajole kids into telling their sad stories and notify the authorities, we force every member of that family to recognize and acknowledge something that he or she has been desperately trying to ignore. Everyone suffers as a result, and it's nearly always the child who assumes most of the guilt.

The way the child usually sees it, it's her fault that the family has been disrupted. If she hadn't complained, Mommy and Daddy would still be together, and everyone could go home. Now what are they going to do without

Daddy's salary? Who is going to take care of them? Where are they going to live? It happens all the time. Some wretched excuse of a parent looks at some sad child, covered with bruises, and says, "Now look at what you've done." Even if she knows better, the child can't help but feel guilty.

The thing most people don't understand about dysfunctional families is that in most cases no one wants to know anything. Even if the home situation is unbearable, many people feel that a horrible family life is better than no family at all. There are plenty of mothers out there who know that their kids are being molested by the man of the house but decide not to rock the boat. In order to keep the "family" together, they pretend that nothing is happening. But when the cops step in, there's no more pretending. The charade is over.

Sometimes a visit from the authorities is only the beginning of the nightmare. If a child is removed from her home and put into a foster home, we have to tell the parents where she is and allow them reasonable visitation rights. If the parent has mental problems or is otherwise disturbed (and what parent who beats his child or has sex with her isn't disturbed?), it's not unusual to see some retaliation against the foster family or the child. The bottom line is that the child is still in danger. Our system of handling child abuse cases is far from perfect.

A few years ago a fellow cop came into the station carrying a little boy who had been standing out in the middle of Van Nuys Boulevard. He was a little thing, about four years old, and he had nearly got himself run over a couple of times. He was scared to death, and that patrol cop—a great big guy, and fierce-looking—didn't make the boy any more relaxed. It took the patrol cop all of ten seconds to turn the child over to me.

I tried to talk to the little boy, but he wouldn't respond, not verbally. I knew it wasn't the language barrier that was coming between us. My Spanish isn't great, but I knew enough to make myself understood. I kept talking to him, hugging him, and giving him fruit punch and ice cream and other treats, but he still wouldn't say anything. I began to think that he *couldn't* talk. After he had been with me for several hours, a little girl, who looked just a couple of years older than he, came into the station and called to him. She told him that it was time to go home, that his mother wanted him. I could tell that he heard what his sister was saying, but he didn't say anything to her, either. He just held on to me as tight as he could.

The impulse to take him home with me was incredibly strong, but of course, I had to take him back to his own home. It turned out that he lived in a little apartment right across the street from the station. When the three of us got there, I found his mother and seven other children living in a couple of rooms. The little boy's mother, who had no husband, was a virtual breeding machine, literally having a baby every year. My little friend was four, and he had three younger siblings. In addition to the six-year-old sister I had already met there were three others, all under the age of ten.

There were no signs of abuse in the house, so I had no business even staying around to talk, but I couldn't tear myself away from the little boy and his family. I stayed around for a couple of hours and tried to get to know them. Before I knew it, I had taken the family on as a project. The first thing I did was find someone to teach the mother about birth control. Then I got the guys at the station to bring in food, clothes, and even a few toys. I used to visit them a couple of times a week, and the little boy stopped in at the station a few times. Once in a while he joined me for Code 7 (lunch). It wasn't much, especially when compared to all those seriously abused kids I couldn't help, but it made me feel good to get involved. The day the little boy finally spoke to me was one I'll never forget.

I READ SOMEWHERE that people who were abused as children are very likely to abuse their own kids when they become adults. I don't doubt the statistics, but I know in my heart that I am an exception. I've never so much as spanked my daughter, and no matter how many horror stories I have listened to, how many times I looked at that child abuse scrapbook, I have yet to be able to fathom how anyone could ever harm a child. I didn't have my daughter until I was in my late thirties, and her appearance was something of a miracle. The first time I held Serina in my arms, I had an overpowering feeling of protectiveness, unlike any emotion I have ever felt or expected to feel in my life. That must be when I lost my "professional objectivity."

POLICE
ACADEMY

*THE MORE YOU SWEAT UP HERE, THE LESS YOU WILL
BLEED ON THE STREET.*
— SIGN POSTED AT THE LOS ANGELES
POLICE ACADEMY

I 've always gotten along great with loonies. Even when I
was a little kid, moving from town to town and being
passed around from family to family, nothing much ever
fazed me. There I was, surrounded by what most "normal"
people would think of as aberrant behavior—mostly in burlesque houses—and not only would I not be bothered by it;
I thoroughly enjoyed the experience. Odd people and mis-
fits have always fascinated me. I'm sure that's one of the
reasons I loved being a cop.

By the time I reached my teens, I was something of an

oddball myself. I went to school, of course, and I was even a pretty fair student, but by the time I graduated from high school, I knew a lot more about nightclubs than I did about pep rallies or organic chemistry. I went on to college, but after finishing three years I still had no idea what I wanted to do when I grew up. With each passing year I felt even more alienated from my fellow students, and I began to wonder if I would ever find a place where I could fit in. That was before I knew that the world's best job for oddballs was the police force.

That's not what the recruiting film said, of course. No, the woman in the film that changed my life said things like, "It's exciting work, and you help people every day" and "It's a wonderful feeling to be a woman who can protect people." It was all silly cheerleader stuff, but it spoke to me. For some reason the idea of joining the police force reached out and grabbed me by the throat and wouldn't let go. This was long before *Kojak* and *Hunter,* not to mention *Cagney and Lacey* and Angie Dickinson in *Police Woman,* so in the absence of a television role model, I had to use my imagination. Fortunately I had enough imagination for a whole police battalion. I wanted to become a cop.

I don't believe that I was power-mad—my interest in joining the force had nothing to do with wanting to tell people what to do—and I didn't do it for the money. In my enthusiasm and naiveté I didn't even know what the job paid when I applied to the Academy. Money has never been an important part of my life. When I found out that the starting salary for cops coming out of the Academy was six hundred dollars a month, I was in heaven. I couldn't believe how lucky I was. (And that was before I found out about overtime!)

No, corny as it sounds, I decided to become a police-woman because I wanted to serve and protect. I thought I could help people and do some good in the world. And I also thought—hoped—that at the ripe old age of twenty-five I might finally have found a place where I really belonged. A family.

I filled out an application for the Police Academy and waited several months for the next scheduled entrance exam. After I got over that hurdle—picture fifteen hundred women huddled in a room for three hours answering every kind of question imaginable—I got a card asking me to come in for an interview, a psychological exam, and a physical fitness test. The oral interview was a breeze, but the physical training test was a killer. (The candidate in front of me dislocated her knee on the hurdles.)

The psychological exam was about what you would expect: ink blots, color analysis, and dozens of questions about whether or not I was afraid of spiders. In the end I was asked to draw a tree. I guess they liked my tree, because I moved on to the next level—the background check. Before they would let any candidate into the Police Academy, they had to make sure that there was no police record, history of drug abuse, or any other undesirable element in his or her past.

I read recently that the LAPD is having some trouble filling its ranks these days. The article said that drug and gang problems are so terrible that most people don't want to join the force anymore. Back when I applied to the Academy, they had more applications than they could handle; the competition for the existing slots was fierce. On my birthday, April 1, 1967, I got the letter I had been anticipating for months: "Your application to the Los Angeles Police Academy has been accepted."

I was *in*.

A FRIEND OF mine recently told me that when she first met me—on our first day in the Los Angeles Police Academy—I reminded her of a mouse, a cute little mouse. She couldn't explain what she meant by that, but I didn't need an explanation. I remember myself that way too, thin, rather timid, more than a little nervous at the prospect of spending the next eight weeks learning how to serve and protect the people of Los Angeles. But that feeling subsided as I settled in. This form of boot camp is designed to keep you on edge, so I can't say I was ever comfortable. But I definitely belonged.

I loved the grounds and the buildings. They are wonderful to look at, formidable and friendly at the same time. There is a feeling of history there. I've been hearing rumblings recently about how they're thinking of tearing the place down and putting up a bigger facility, but I truly hope that doesn't happen.

There were ten women in my Police Academy class—remember, this was the Dark Ages—and about two hundred men. All the women were in their late twenties or early thirties, older than the men, and many were switching careers in midstream, from nursing, teaching, and secretarial work, to name a few. When it came time for parties, students were allowed to mix with the opposite sex, but otherwise the men and women were completely segregated. All of our classes were separate—we did juvenile detective procedures while the guys learned how to work traffic reports—and fraternization was strictly forbidden. I never did hear a convincing argument for this rule.

The work at the Academy was hard, but I loved that, too. It was certainly a lot more interesting than the three years of college I had gone through. Each day was divided into thirds—classroom study, physical training, and skills. In the classroom we made our way through a detailed three-page syllabus: Introduction to Law Enforcement, Police Community Relations, Introduction to Law, Laws of Evidence, Criminal Investigation, Communications, and dozens of other topics. We studied the psychology of criminals and victims, learned how the police department functions, and talked about how the city was laid out. I thought I really knew my way around Los Angeles before I started at the Academy, but the cop's-eye view of the city—division by division—gave me a whole new perspective. (Other cities, such as New York, have precincts; L.A. has divisions.)

We memorized terminology and studied our new Bible—the LAPD Field Manual. It was like taking a Berlitz course in an interesting foreign language and a lot more exciting than second-year French. I was fascinated by everything. We studied street gangs the way Margaret Mead studied

Samoa—names, colors, most popular hangouts, archene-mies, weapons of choice. I no longer have the alphabetized gang list we were given back then, but I have the one that was distributed in 1989. There are forty-nine gang names on it, a lot of them new to me, such as the Adidas Boys, the Anti-Fag League, and (my favorite) the Mickey Mouse Club.

In our skills sessions we learned self-defense and tactics, and we got to know how to use the equipment that eventu-ally would be assigned to us—with special emphasis on guns. We learned to shoot, of course, but not until we had been thoroughly trained on the different kinds of guns, how each of them works, and how to clean each and every one of them so that it gleamed. The training was sometimes tedi-ous and amazingly thorough, but there was a very good reason behind every element of the weaponry classes.

Without a doubt, physical training was the hardest part of my life at the Academy. To this day if I so much as see a hurdle, I break out into a cold sweat. (A friend of mine who fought in Vietnam said that when he was over there, marching through the wet muck with a twenty-pound pack on his back, he swore that he would never, *ever*, go on a hike again, even in Muir Woods on a clear day. That's how I feel about jumping.) In addition to those dreaded hurdles there were vigorous calisthenics for an hour each day, and we had to run everywhere—uphill, downhill, all over campus, miles each day, even in ninety-degree heat. Today the re-cruits wear fatigues, but in those days we were a vision in sweatpants and sweatshirts. Shorts were too provocative, we were told.

Physical fitness was one area in which men and women were created equal; we were worked just as hard and just as long as the guys. There were days when the pushing, prodding, and taunting were almost too much to bear, but there was no point in looking for sympathy. The attitude of the people in charge was: we want you to be tough. If you can't take it, you can leave. Some people did just that, but not in my class. We all made it, maybe because we helped each other and found ways to laugh at it all.

We had our share of field trips as well, which were a nice break from the routine. I always looked forward to a day or two away from classes on Courtroom Demeanor or Evidence Seizure Concepts, not to mention those hurdles. One day we learned about Courtroom Demeanor firsthand when we watched police officers testify in court. Another time we were given a tour of the morgue. I had always heard about how horrifying the morgue was supposed to be, so I walked in fully prepared to get sick or pass out when I viewed my first autopsy—some poor guy in his mid-forties had been stabbed, and not very neatly at that—but I was mesmerized by the whole process. Some of my classmates didn't fare quite so well. One woman fainted, and a couple never actually got their eyes open.

As I learned later, the only dead bodies that really bothered me when I was on the job were those of the kids. With adults I found that I could detach myself when I was working; concentrating on gathering evidence and asking questions, I forgot to think about the person that the corpse used to be. The cop part of me would take over, and the civilian part would shut down.

When victims were still breathing, the blood and gore were a lot tougher to take in stride, as I discovered when our class took a late-night outing to the emergency room of the nearby hospital. It was your typical Saturday night crowd— one gunshot wound, two drug overdoses, and a small kid who had caught his hand in a stroller. We all felt a little queasy when we left.

Toward the end of our eight-week training, we would also spend some time out in the field with full-time police officers—to get our feet wet. My tour of duty was spent in the Georgia Street Juvenile Division. The building looked like an old-fashioned grammar school—one of those sweet brick schoolhouses you sometimes see in small towns in the Midwest—but there was nothing sweet about the neighborhood.

I was assigned to the J car—J for Juvenile—with a training officer named Mike, who was and is a great guy. He didn't seem to mind having to babysit a trainee, even when I asked too many stupid questions. I didn't really talk much in those early days. I was a little shy and self-conscious, and besides, I had enough to do just to watch Mike.

The first thing I noticed about Mike was that he saw *everything*. Even when he appeared to be chatting or explaining one of the fine points of police work or just driving aimlessly around the neighborhood, his eyes were in constant motion, checking out everybody and everything. All cops do that. Another thing they do is listen. The police radio is on all the time, and there's constant noise, much of it nearly incomprehensible unless you know what to listen for and how to speak the language. It takes practice to speak "radio-ese," and Mike was an expert. I could be telling him one of the funniest jokes in the world, and if a call for us came over the radio, he would hear it.

One day at around four o'clock, an hour into our shift, Mike suddenly put the car in gear and took off like a shot. I had no idea why, but as he drove, he explained—patiently, as always. There had been a call on the radio—"J car number sixty-four, we have a Code Four-five-nine," the voice said, and gave the address—and Mike was moving in response. A burglary was in progress, and we were on our way there in a big hurry.

I don't think I've ever been so excited and scared at the same time. "What the hell am I doing here?" was one of the many things that ran through my mind as we raced through the streets. Another was, "Please don't let anything happen." When we got to the address, Mike was incredibly calm. He told me what he was going to do and gave me my instructions. I didn't say a word; I just concentrated on following his orders exactly and as quickly as I could. His icy calmness must have been contagious, because my heart was no longer somewhere up in my throat. My breathing was almost normal.

It turned out that a bunch of kids, six of them in their late teens, were in the process of stealing a car. Mike and I pulled up across the street from them and got out of the J car. Mike walked toward them, and just as he was about to reach them, one of the kids made a gesture as if he was going to pull a gun on Mike. Without hesitating, I pulled my gun out and told the kid to stop where he was. "Don't move a muscle," I said, and kept my gun pointed right at him. Mike quickly snatched the kid's gun away—he was reaching for one after all!—and we took the burglars to the station.

When we were back out in the J car again, Mike told me I had done my job perfectly. I was thrilled. What thrilled me even more, though, was knowing that I hadn't hesitated to do what had to be done. My feet were officially wet.

GRADUATION IS SOMETHING of a blur in my memory now. All I can recall with complete clarity is how happy I was that I was finally going to be a policewoman. The ceremony itself was low-key but lovely. The Academy put the hurdles in storage for the day and set up bleachers on the athletic field, and we all—men and women together this time—marched out onto the grass in our brand new dress uniforms. Women wore high heels and white gloves and our official police-woman's shoulder bags. The gun in my bag banged heavily against my hip.

A band played, the mayor and the chief of police congratulated us and shook our hands, and the television cameras rolled. My mother, who sat in the bleachers with a few of her friends, couldn't have been prouder; after all, she had known cops nearly all of her life, and she liked most of them. (She had a surprise party planned for after the ceremony. We were all going over to celebrate at the Magic Castle, a nightclub where she used to work, and a magician was going to carve a badge out of a bar of soap.) All in all, it was a fitting end and a great beginning.

I don't recall the commencement address we listened to

that day, but I do remember some words of wisdom I heard just a few days earlier. They came from one of my female training officers, Sergeant Connie Speck, a cop who had been on the job almost fifteen years. "Being a cop is like being a garage mechanic," she explained. "Once you're comfortable with the job and know what you're doing, it's no more dangerous than working on a car with the engine running. You'll be fine as long as you don't put your hand anywhere near the fan."

With that, I figured I was as ready as I was ever going to be. I didn't feel like a real policewoman yet. But at least I wasn't a cute little mouse anymore.

JAILHOUSE
ROCK

Arrestees shall be searched at the booking desk in accordance with the law. . . . Note: Employees conducting a strip search or visual body cavity search shall not touch the breasts, buttocks, or genitalia of the arrestee.

—FROM THE 1989 LAPD FIELD MANUAL
(RULE 620.10)

Back in the fifties, when my mother was a headliner on the burlesque circuit, she had a theory about performing that I've never forgotten. "People always remember the first couple of minutes of your act and the last couple of minutes of your act," she told me. "Give them a good beginning and a strong finish, and they'll always go home happy."

I've thought about her theory many times throughout my life, but never more than on my first day of work on the police force. People who were on the job back then are *still* talking about the entrance I made. The year was 1967, and I, an eager rookie fresh out of the Police Academy, was assigned to the Van Nuys Jail.

I was incredibly excited and nervous about being a policewoman and about getting this assignment—I was going to be a jailer!—so excited, in fact, that I didn't pay quite enough attention to the instructions they gave us about what to wear and what to do when we reported for work. That first day I got up hours early and dressed with great care. I put on my navy blue skirt, my dress shirt, and my dress tie. I had already slipped on the sheerest stockings I could find, which looked great with my shiny new high heels. My hair was arranged in a flawless bouffant, which set off my cap to perfection. My nails and makeup looked as if a professional had done them. Just before I left the house, I cleaned my gun one last time and put it, fully loaded, in my neat but bulky policewoman's purse. I was ready for *work*.

When I got to the station, I drove my beat-up little car up the ramp and left it where all the police cars were parked. As I got out of the car and started walking proudly toward the front door of the station—head up, chest out, stomach in—I could see that three floors of cops were staring out their windows at me, but I pretended not to notice them. I had no idea of what they were looking at, so I acted as nonchalant as I could manage and walked briskly over to the front door of the station. "I've been doing this every day for years" was the casual effect I was striving for.

Once I got in the station, people continued to ogle me. No

one said anything, so I kept on marching purposefully, toward the main desk of the jail, with all eyes on me every step of the way. It was incredibly quiet; all I could hear was the clicking of my newly polished high heels on the cement floor. Still pretending to be completely at home, I kept walking.

When I got to the jail entrance, there were prisoners lined up on either side of the hall, all in handcuffs, and even *they* stared at me. I said hello to the sergeant, identified myself, and told him I was reporting for duty. That's when the snickering started. First only a few people laughed, but before long nearly everyone, including the prisoners, joined in the hilarity. When there was a lull in the laughter, Sergeant Korea, a veteran who had seen it all in his day, looked long and hard at me and said, so that everyone could hear, "What the hell are *you* supposed to be? A fuckin' *stewardess*?"

The place went crazy. Everybody in the entire police station cracked up at once. For a moment I gave serious thought to turning and slinking away, but I decided to laugh instead. "Coffee, tea, or milk?" was all I could think of to say.

It turns out that I had done *everything* wrong. First of all, I wasn't supposed to wear my dress uniform. Jailers had a different outfit, which I had been told about but was too keyed up to hear: black tie shoes, a long-sleeved blue shirt, and a black skirt—no tie, no hat, no bouffant hairdo, and certainly no high heels. So much for my stewardess look. Second of all, I wasn't supposed to park my nonregulation car with the police cars: "civilian" cars went in a lot across the way. Third, I wasn't meant to enter through the front door. Finally, the worst thing that anyone working in a jail can do is bring in a loaded gun. No weapons at all are allowed in there.

Well, I was a little late getting started that first day. I had to change into a jailer outfit that someone loaned me, including shoes, turn in my gun, and move my car before punching in. But at least I'd made my mark. And my second day on the job went without a hitch. No one ever has to teach me anything twice.

The Van Nuys Jail, where I was to spend the better part of the next two years (with time out to work undercover for Homicide, Vice, and a special abortion detail), was a holding jail, a place where transient prisoners were held for a night or two until they raised money for bail or were called before a judge. No one was there for very long—except me, of course. (Once in a while when a prisoner complained about having to stay there, I'd respond by saying, "Hey, you're going to be out of here in two days. I've been here for two years.") Practically no one spent more than three days with us, five at the most.

The jail held over two hundred people, with the men on one side and the women on the other. Usually we stuck with our own kind—women supervising women, men guarding men—but occasionally I would be sent over to work the men's side. Everything over there was the same except that I didn't have to search the men prisoners. (Regulations said that prisoners were to be searched by a police officer of the same gender.) The lieutenant in charge of both sides of the jail was, naturally, a man.

When a prisoner was brought in to us by a detective or some other arresting officer, the first stop was a big electric door at the entrance to the jail, where police officers checked their guns. Then the prisoner was taken down a hall past the interview rooms, the camera room, and another little door that leads into the nurse's office. There's a nurse on duty twenty-four hours a day now, but back when I started, we had no such luxury. We didn't even have aspirin. If prisoners complained of pain, we gave them sugar pills, which was all we had in the "dispensary." The funny thing was, those placebos worked almost every time.

When the arresting officer and the prisoner reached my desk, the paperwork for booking would begin: I'd record name, address, phone number, and the name of the arresting officer and describe the charge. Then I'd go through the standard questions:

"Are you ill or injured?"

"Are you under the care of a doctor?"

"Do you have epilepsy, diabetes, or tuberculosis?"

"Are you pregnant?"

"Do you have a venereal disease?"

There were many more questions like those, and any *yes* answer had to be dealt with before we could proceed to the fingerprinting and—my least favorite part of life in the jail—the search.

Every prisoner coming into the jail had to be searched. Most times we would just pat them down and take away

anything that wasn't allowed, which was just about everything. All we left them were the clothes they had on, ten
dollars in cash (unless the person was too stoned or drunk
to watch out for the money herself, in which case we allowed
her only two dollars), cigarettes, a handkerchief, a rubber or
plastic comb, a hearing aid, prescription eyeglasses, and the
citation that explained why she was there in the first place.

Most of the time a routine search was all that was called
for, but when the prisoner was charged with a felony or if
the case had anything to do with narcotics, I had to do a skin
search. We've all heard a lot about how demeaning a strip
search is for a prisoner—and every word of it is true—but
I'm here to tell you that a strip search is no day at the beach
for the jailer either. I've seen some pretty gamy things in my
day, which is why I never went into the strip-search room
without my little sample bottles of perfume. Before searching the female prisoners, I'd hold a bottle of perfume right
under my nose. Sometimes even that didn't help.

As I said, in the jail women police officers search women
prisoners, and male officers search the men. If there's any
doubt about the gender of the prisoner, a female police
officer does the search. One afternoon a woman was brought
into the jail for shoplifting. She was a knockout: tall and
statuesque, with a beautiful face flawlessly made up, long
blond hair, and wearing an expensive-looking green leather
outfit. At first glance she looked like a model. At second
glance—when you had time to see the huge Adam's apple
she had—she looked like a man.

I noticed it right away, but I didn't say anything. She

could have been a transsexual, which would mean she was officially a woman. The truth came out during the search. That's when I discovered that the prisoner was wearing falsies and had curled his cock down between his legs and taped it in place. He was officially a man and had to be locked up on the other side. He begged me to keep his secret; afraid of what would happen to him in a men's prison, he desperately wanted to be kept with the women. I felt really sorry for him, but I had no choice. I had to turn him over to the guys.

Because of the kind of jail Van Nuys was, virtually every kind of criminal imaginable crossed our threshold, from pickpockets and purse snatchers to murderers and mobsters who were under police protection. I discovered very early on that everything in the jail went in cycles, depending on the weather, the time of day, and the time of year. First thing in the morning we got people who've been picked up on old warrants. Around four o'clock in the afternoon the shoplifters would be brought in. Vagrants spent a lot of the rainy season with us, but when the sun came out, so did the weenie wavers, the men brought in for indecent exposure. From nine in the evening until two in the morning we mostly saw hookers. It got so I didn't need either a watch or a calendar to tell me what time of the day or year it was. When I worked the jail, I always knew.

My favorite prisoners were the hookers. They had the most interesting stories and were the easiest to handle. Most of them didn't even seem to mind being in prison for a couple of hours. I think they were just happy to be off their feet and get a little rest. I was always glad when the hookers in the jail felt like talking, because then I had a chance to gather information. I knew that one day I was going to be working undercover for Vice, and any advance research I could do would come in handy. To me those conversations were a little like interrogation, only there was a lot more laughing. I started with the easy stuff, about where they bought their clothes and how they came to choose to wear a certain dress or pair of shoes. Then I'd move on to what part of town they worked in and how much they charged for various services. Along the way I'd pay special attention to the language they used. It wasn't enough to know what was going on out there and to look the part. If I was going to be a convincing hooker, I had to sound like one, and that meant knowing the latest street talk. Eventually we got around to the subject of pimps, as in what they did for—and to—the hookers. Most of the women would admit how much they hated their pimps, but they would never acknowledge their addiction to them. It was in jail that I started despising pimps. I don't think those hookers ever knew they were being "interrogated" as we talked and laughed and gossiped through the night. I tried to make them comfortable, and I think I succeeded. For one thing, I usually let them make all the phone calls they wanted.

Of course, not all prisoners were content to sit around and tell fascinating stories all night. Many of them liked to while away the hours calling us names. No police officer on any beat is a stranger to verbal abuse, but the jail has to be the worst. After a couple of months in there I regarded

"Motherfuckin' Dyke Pig" as my middle name. Most of the time I didn't let the name-calling get to me, but every once in a while, especially if I was really tired, it would get on my nerves. I'd ask them to at least call me something new. That would slow down the barrage of insults—for about thirty seconds.

The name-calling was a genuine pleasure compared to the physical abuse that most of us had to endure in the jail. It seems strange now to think that the most dangerous assignment I ever had on the police force was also my first assignment, the jail. Police officers who work the holding jail are in constant danger. Unarmed and outnumbered by prisoners, they're always running the risk of getting stabbed or strangled or jumped from behind. That's why searches are so important.

There was some kind of fight (we were supposed to call them *altercations*) on nearly every shift—the night shift was the worst, by far—and those cement floors didn't do much to cushion the impact when we were thrown. For years I was never without some kind of bruise on my tailbone from an "altercation." I begged the people in charge to put in rubber mats, at least in the fingerprinting area, which is where most of the altercations took place, but it didn't happen. I was never badly hurt, glad to say, but plenty of other people were. One night a friend of mine got thrown across the room and landed on her tailbone so hard that she ended up on permanent disability. Her days of police work were over almost before they began.

Because we weren't armed, the only things we could

count on were our strength and our smarts. Most of us were pretty fit—regulations demanded it—but some of those prisoners were a lot stronger, especially if they were on drugs. We had to be on our guard at all times, even when the prisoner seemed like a meek little thing. When I was first assigned to the jail, I used to wear my hair up in a bun—very tidy, very official-looking, I thought—but I soon found out that my bun was actually a "handle" for the prisoners, who would grab it and use it to throw me around. The first thing a prisoner reaches for during an altercation is a handful of hair. When I figured that out, I started wearing wigs to work, which added an element of surprise to my end of an altercation. I used to enjoy seeing the stunned expressions on the prisoners' faces when the handful of hair they grabbed came right off my head. (My extensive wig collection came in handy later when I worked hookers.)

The closest call I ever had came just a few weeks before I was scheduled to leave the jail and be reassigned. An arresting officer had brought his prisoner in and then left the two of us alone, standing on the outside of the cage. I thought that she had already been searched—she should have been before she got to me—but I noticed that she still had her earrings on.

"Take off the earrings," I told her.

"Fuck you," she replied.

"Sorry, there's no jewelry allowed in the jail," I explained. "You'll get your earrings back when you leave."

"Fuck you," she answered.

"Look," I said, trying to be patient with her, "you're better off giving the earrings to me and letting me hold them for you. If you wear them in here, somebody is going to steal them from you."

This time she didn't say, "Fuck you." This time she pulled out a knife.

I knew I didn't have the energy to fight her for the knife, and that her first blow was inevitable. I turned my head, closed my eyes, and tightened my stomach muscles. Then I waited for her to stab me and hoped she wouldn't hit anything vital. I had screwed up. I'd been working for fourteen days straight without a break, and I was exhausted—dangerously exhausted.

There were other people not too far away, but they were busily typing or filing or trading gossip and they didn't know what was happening. Even if they had known, they couldn't have helped me in time. So I stood there, eyes closed and stomach tight, waiting for this prisoner to give her best shot. What happened then was . . . nothing. When I finally opened my eyes and looked over at the prisoner, still holding her knife, she just grinned at me.

"Gotcha," she said, and handed me the knife.

"Fuck you," I answered—believe me, that was as witty as I could be at the time—and took it. I needed the rest of the shift to stop shaking.

One of the most frightening experiences I ever had in the Van Nuys Jail had nothing to do with an altercation or even a prisoner. It took place on the night shift, which had always been my favorite. There were no prisoners in the jail that night—that happened only a few times in my time there—and the only person I had for company was Lulu, the jail orderly. Lulu and I had always got along very well; we were always teasing each other and arguing about which of us had the harder job. Well, there we were, all alone in the jail, when a huge storm suddenly knocked out all the electricity in that big empty jail. Lulu and I were quite a pair; I was terrified of the dark, and she was terrified of thunder and lightning. We did the only thing we could think of to be safe: We locked ourselves into a cell and spent the night there, wide awake.

I DON'T TALK about it much, but throughout my life I've always had something of a sixth sense. Some call it intuition, some ESP, others radar or a hunch. Many cops have it and file it under the general category of street smarts. One of those intuitions came to me while I was working the Van Nuys Jail.

Two detectives brought in a woman they had arrested for forgery. Like a lot of forgers, she was a nice-looking middle-class woman, very well dressed, and the detectives were being very polite, almost courtly to her. She was supposed to be in handcuffs at this point, but they hadn't cuffed her. She was a tiny thing—barely five two—and she was behaving like Blanche DuBois in *A Streetcar Named Desire*. I fully expected her to tell the detectives that she had always depended on the kindness of strangers. She was carrying a small brown purse.

When they brought her to my desk, I surveyed the scene,

and I thought to myself, "Boy, have you got these guys snowed, honey." And all of a sudden I knew it: there was a gun in that little brown purse, and it was loaded. Alarms were ringing in my head.

My next thought was, "How am I gonna get this gun away from her? These guys are acting as if she's their best friend."

I decided to take the direct approach.

"Rules are rules, guys," I told them, smiling as pleasantly as I could. Looking at her I said, "I'll take your purse."

She smiled back at me reassuringly and said, "You don't have to search me. I'm bailing right out."

I walked toward her. No sudden movements, still friendly. "While you're our guest, I *do* have to search you. Hand me the purse, please."

The detectives were busy talking about a boxing match, reviewing punches with each other. As far as they were concerned, their female prisoner was my "ladies' work." I looked at the woman—who was now acting more like Queen Victoria than Blanche DuBois—and said, "Give it to me *now!*"

"I don't have to give you anything, you fucking bitch!" she shouted.

At last the detectives smelled a rat. As she screamed and started to yank her purse out of my reach, they grabbed her arm. When they finally cuffed her, I opened the purse, reached in, and pulled out a small handgun. They almost crapped in their pants when they saw it.

IN ALL MY years on the force I don't think a month went by
without someone coming up to me and saying, "Are you the
one who got in trouble with the banana in the jail?"

Yes, that was me.

It was 1970 and I was working the late shift with three
other policewomen. There wasn't much action that night;
the jail was almost empty. We were all bored. So we did
what we always did; we talked about men. One of my partners liked to take official sex surveys whenever it got slow.
That night, she was asking if any of us "swallowed" when
the subject of how to give good head came up.

One of the other women—I'll call her Mary—was single,
shy, and had fallen hard for a lieutenant. Mary was determined to win his heart. She thought the way to victory was
to be more exciting in bed. For some reason I decided to
help Mary with her problem. If she found me a banana, I
told her, I'd demonstrate the finer points of fellatio. (I had
recently been given a few pointers myself from some hookers who were temporary guests.) Someone said that in order
to learn to do it for the lieutenant she should probably
practice with a thimble.

Personal statistics aside, within minutes someone had
located a banana, and I kept my end of the bargain. A few
minutes into my class on Oral Sex 101, I noticed that there
were a few red faces in the room and Mary wore a strange
expression. Figuring that they were just a little embarrassed, I didn't give their reactions much thought. My train-

ing officer looked especially stricken, but I figured it was because she was gay and sort of put off by the whole idea of sex with a man.

As I warmed to my topic—"Remember, if he starts to lose his erection, all you have to do is press right here"—I noticed that I was losing my audience. They were staring not at me and my banana but at something—or someone— directly behind me. I stopped my demonstration and glanced over my shoulder. Sure enough, my lieutenant had come into the room, and it turned out that he had been standing there watching me nearly the whole time. Too bad it wasn't Mary's lieutenant. Perhaps he would have understood, though I've never met any lieutenant who would have had much of a sense of humor about that scene. Unfortunately, this guy was one of the starchiest, most spit-and-polish lieutenants who's ever been on any police force anywhere. He was *definitely* not amused.

I looked around the room and saw the horrified expressions of my colleagues. Mary looked as if she wanted to evaporate, and my training officer's expression was almost as bad. But no one could help me now. I was on my own.

The lieutenant's eyes burned holes through me, but even so, I couldn't help but see the humor in the situation. And I proceeded to make matters even worse.

"Good evening, Lieutenant," I said cheerfully. Then I slowly peeled the banana and ate it. Without saying a word he turned on his heel and stormed out. In the end, Mary got her man (maybe she learned something) and I got a reprimand. No one ever said life was fair.

IN THE YEARS I worked the jail I never met anyone who was guilty. We could have all the evidence in the world piled up against someone, and she would still claim that she was totally and completely innocent. When I first worked there, I came across one of my all-time favorite cases of denial. I was searching a woman and found narcotics in her bra. I took out the little bags of cocaine from her size 34C Maidenform, tossed them to the arresting narcotics officer, and gave her a meaningful look.

"Look what I found," I said.

"That's *not* my bra," the woman responded.

That was the first of many, many times I heard that claim.

Not everybody I came across in the jail made me smile as much as she did, but I loved it anyhow, partly because the jail was my first assignment on the force but also because it got me off to a running start. I learned a lot in a hurry. The classes and the theories and the simulated crimes of the Police Academy had been useful, but I didn't become a real cop until the jail. That's when my training truly kicked in. Role-playing is nothing compared to the real thing. The fights in the jail were *real.* In the jail I was exposed to a cross-section of criminal life without having to go out and look for it. It came to me. I've often thought that everyone on the force should start off in the jail. If nothing else, it gives a cop a preview of coming attractions.

When I left the jail, I didn't go very far geographically— as a matter of fact, I stayed in the same building—but in terms of assignments, I traveled a long, long way. One day I was doing strip searches and talking shop with hookers in the jail. The next day I was working in Community Relations, where my job description included giving speeches about safety, talking to children about not taking candy from strangers, going to luncheons, and generally comporting myself like a politician who's up for reelection. I did everything but kiss babies.

To say it was a big adjustment for me is a gross understatement. It took me quite a while after leaving the jail to relate to people, especially women, in a normal way. I couldn't help it; every woman I met was a potential prisoner. By the time I left the jail, when I saw a woman wearing jewelry, it never occurred to me to admire it. All I could think was, "Shit, look how tight that ring is. I'll *never* get it off her. And those earrings! I'll bet she hasn't washed her ears in months!"

Yes, it was *definitely* time to move on.

WORKING HOOKERS

Civilian clothing worn by an employee while on duty shall be appropriate to his assignment.

—FROM THE 1989 LAPD FIELD MANUAL (RULE 605.50)

When I was a little girl, I used to dream about growing up and going on the stage. I suppose that my mother's glamorous career as a burlesque dancer had a lot to do with my dream. In college I went out for musical productions and loved every minute of them. Anyhow, I *knew* that I was going to be a *great* actress. It turns out that I was right. The only thing is, I ended up doing my acting for the Los Angeles Police Department.

Today, of course, all cops are created equal, but back in the late 1960s, when I first came on the job, most of the really interesting police assignments were reserved for men. Only men could work Homicide or Metro, for instance. Women were mostly relegated to Juvenile, the jail, or Community Relations. One of the few exciting jobs a woman *could* get assigned to was Vice. When it comes to passing themselves off as hookers, men just don't have what it takes.

Back then we called the detail "working hookers." Today the LAPD Field Manual refers to it more formally—as the Trick Task Force. ("Tricks" are what prostitutes call their customers, though I suppose anyone who watches television or goes to the movies already knows that.) The work is still the same, however, and the cast of characters hasn't changed very much at all.

I was never assigned to Vice full-time, but for the twenty years I was on the job I was loaned out regularly to the Trick Task Force. When my regular job was working the desk, I made it a rule never to stay put for too long a stretch. I didn't mind it for a time—in fact, I almost enjoyed it—but eventually I'd get bored with taking reports and handling the public and juggling phone calls, and I'd start bugging my sergeant to find out if some other unit could use me. In some instances I'd hear about a specific case—often a rape—and put in a bid to be assigned there. And whenever I needed a little excitement in my life, I'd volunteer to work Vice. As anyone who has ever worked with me would be glad to tell you, I don't like to hear the word no. So I was always getting loaned out to other units.

When I worked Vice, sometimes I'd stay as long as a month. Other times I'd be out just for a night or a weekend with the Trick Task Force. The short assignments were usually to scout complaints, when the guys assigned to a case couldn't decide whether it made sense to move a hooker detail into a new area. They would send me out there to see what I could see. They also used me to train newcomers to the force in the lively art of working hookers. Having the new recruits spend a couple of nights out on the streets was a lot more useful than screening a month's worth of training films. Sometimes they brought me in to persuade some of the new women to give the work a try.

Over the years I've met plenty of women on the force who refused to work hookers. Some were put off by the court time or the long hours. Some were afraid of the danger. All those reactions are perfectly understandable, but most of the people who wouldn't do it had a different reason: they thought that the work was beneath their dignity. "I'm not gonna work this sleazy job. I didn't join the force to go out on the street and pretend to be a prostitute," they'd say, and it took some convincing to change their minds. Some never did come around.

I've never felt that working hookers was anything but the most honorable work, and it always gave me tremendous satisfaction to do it well. To me the most important job a cop can do is to put bad guys in jail, and when I worked hookers, I did that, in spades. The guys told me that I was one of the best they had on the Trick Task Force, and I was proud of that. It gave me a heady feeling to be out there shaking things up, and I enjoyed that element of danger. It also gave me a chance to work on my acting technique and wear some pretty outrageous clothes. Anytime I could manage it, I tried to have fun out there.

Getting dressed for a night of working hookers was a real trip. In the old days I used to choose my outfits by myself, but for the last five or six years my daughter helped me get ready. I almost always stayed away from the sleazy and the tacky—no Spandex or fishnet stockings or micro-miniskirts for me. I wanted to be a good-looking prostitute. When I was just starting out on the force, I read something that has stayed with me all these years; some psychologists determined that the better-looking you are, the more comfortable people are with you, and the more comfortable people are with you, the more likely they are to be communicative. Since the business of the Trick Task Force was to make people want to communicate, I always did my best to look good on the street.

Twenty years ago policewomen dressed a lot more provocatively than they do today on the Trick Task Force, but then so did the prostitutes themselves. It used to be spangles and feathers, push-up bras and false eyelashes, five-inch heels and a lot of flashy accessories. Prostitutes wanted to attract attention, and so did cops who were posing as hookers. My standard outfit back then was spike heels, a red or black wig, and one of several sexy but simple dresses. One of my absolute favorites was a sleeveless black silk turtleneck sheath that came just a few inches below my ass. I'd finish off the outfit with some flashy earrings and, sometimes, a flowing cape. I used to make special trips over to an out-of-the-way neighborhood in Hollywood to buy my hooker clothes. Back when I was starting out, one of the pimps on Sepulveda Boulevard gave me the street name Sweetcheeks. To this day one of my prized possessions is a pair of jeans with SWEETCHEEKS spelled out in rhinestones across the rear end.

Today the LAPD is concerned that their undercover Vice cops will be accused of entrapment, so they have to blend in with the rest of the scenery. Toward the end of my tenure on the force I would usually go out in tight jeans, a cutoff sweatshirt, and my Indian boots—the standard hooker outfit of the late 1980s. I wouldn't wear much makeup—I opted for the fresh-scrubbed look—and I'd let my hair fly wild and loose. There were lots of nights when I looked as proper and tidy as any other ordinary person walking around on the street. If I was going to be out on the streets for several nights, I changed my look each night, wearing different wigs and changing outfits. I tried not to look the same two nights in a row.

One accessory I always wore was my trademark hat, a big black cowboy hat with a silver band. It looked pretty good on me if I do say so myself, but I didn't wear it because of the way I looked. I used the hat to signal the guys who were working with me. When I took my hat off, that told them I had the "elements" I needed to make an arrest. For the crime of solicitation the elements weren't all that complicated. I had to have proof that the trick wanted sex of some variety or another, that he wanted to pay me, and how much money was going to change hands. I had to be able to prove that there was no enticement or entrapment; I couldn't trick him into making the offer by anything I said or did, which was fine with me. The trick had to make the offer voluntarily. When my hat came off, it was time for my coworkers to make their move.

Through the years I've worked hookers all over the city, but I've spent most of my time in Hollywood, Van Nuys, North Hollywood, and the Valley. Probably the hottest of all hot spots is Sepulveda Boulevard in Van Nuys; there is more prostitution on that street than anywhere else in the city of Los Angeles. People come from all over the globe to get laid on Sepulveda, or at least that's how it seems. Because the area is filled with transients, we could have worked that street all day every day and never stopped arresting people. You would think that the AIDS epidemic would have slowed down the hooker activity, but as far as I can tell, it's had no effect whatsoever on sex for sale.

A typical night of working hookers would start at ten o'clock. I'd put on my outfit, drive over to the division in charge of the operation, and get my picture taken. That way there wouldn't be any arguments later about how I was dressed when I went out on the street and whether I had enticed the john to proposition me. Then I'd meet the officers in charge of the assignment and we'd spend some time talking about how we were going to work it.

We'd discuss strategy and officer safety (there was always someone to remind me that I was not supposed to get in a car with a trick and drive off somewhere) and decide what my signal was going to be when I had the elements of the crime. There would usually be a schematic drawing of the area for us to look at, so that we could decide where my partner would be, where the black-and-white police car would be stationed, and where I would take the tricks once I had all the elements. (The actual arrest was always made off the street, so that my cover wasn't blown.) I'd try on my wire and make sure the equipment was working perfectly. Everything that was said by me and the tricks would be monitored and recorded by the team.

Once we had reviewed the rules of the game, we drove to the site and got in position. Then, when the officer in charge of the detail gave me the word, it was time for me to do my stuff. Sometimes I'd just stand on the street, but more often I'd walk slowly, against the traffic. When a john drove up and got my attention—usually he'd say something like, "How much?" or perhaps, "What are you doin' tonight?" or, "Where are you going?" A few would start with, "Can I give you a ride?"

I had a hundred stock responses, but the one that usually worked best was, "Hey, baby, I'm not hitchhiking. And I'm not out here for my health. If you have something to say, say it. If you don't, fuck off."

From there it didn't take long to get to "Fine, how much?"

"That depends on what you want. Talk to me," I'd say.

Then, if the trick hesitated, I'd push it a little. "Hey, if you're gonna talk to me, talk to me. Otherwise get your ass outta here. I'm busy."

I may have *looked* nice out there, but I always acted meaner than shit, even twenty years ago, when I first started out. I had two reasons. One, nobody was *ever* able to accuse me of enticement; there was *nothing* enticing about my attitude toward a john. And two, I really wanted to scare those guys. I came on strong because I wanted them to get lost. If you're nice to these jerks, they can be dangerous. I'd seen too many hookers who had been maimed or killed by some crazy trick—cigarette burns, slashed faces, and a lot worse—and anything I could do to put those nuts out of commission seemed like a good idea to me.

There was a third reason for what one of my partners used to call "Gayleen's Famous Fuck-You Attitude," and that was that it made me feel a hell of a lot better about what I was doing. I wasn't out there saying, "Here I am. Come and get it." I was saying, "What do you want? If you want it, go for it. If you don't want it, get the fuck outta here."

Occasionally the initial conversation with a john would take as long as five or ten minutes, but most of the time I had him signed, sealed, and delivered in a minute or even less. People who want to buy sex don't usually stand on ceremony. When I decided I had enough to make the arrest, I would tell the trick I had a room around the corner and what the room number was. Then I'd explain that I was going to walk over there right now, and when he showed up, I'd give him everything he wanted. That's when I took off my hat. When the guy got to where I sent him, well out of sight of any other johns or hookers, he was arrested.

I worked hookers for twenty years, on and off, and I think that the most shocking thing about it is how little things have changed out there. There are some differences, of course. The lingo hasn't stayed the same, for instance. In the old days the tricks would cruise up and say, "Do you wanna have sex?" Now they're more likely to kick things off with "Do you wanna party?" Code names for the different sex acts have gone through some major changes too. But the price for a blow job has gone from twenty-five dollars down to fifteen. I'm not sure what that says about society—or taste—except that it doesn't make hooking seem like a very promising profession, does it?

People are generally a lot more suspicious these days than they used to be. Nobody trusts anyone; the hookers think that every john is a cop, and the johns think that the hookers are all policewomen. Some of the conversations that result are hilarious, with a lot of people trying to say what they want to say without actually saying it. There were times when trying to get a trick to give me the elements was like pulling weeds in the garden, and stubborn weeds at that. In the end, though, I would almost always get what I needed to make a bust.

Julie, one of my women friends on the force, told me a story about the night her cover was blown by a pimp. A pimp walked right up to her and asked if she'd give him a head job. Trying to get the elements, she said, "How much?" And he said, "Twenty-five cents, Officer Friendly." She never worked hookers again. Another friend of mine, Dorothy, had an even better experience. When she was working Hollywood one night, a trick she arrested turned out to be a famous basketball star. Now *that* was a damned interesting arrest report. Cops are always interested to see what happens in the media when they arrest a celebrity.

Things are a lot more dangerous today too. Twenty years ago we didn't have the same degree of violence there is out there now. Oh, hookers have always been beaten up on the streets, but these days the violence is much more intense. In some of the seamier parts of town we had a lot of whores getting mutilated and killed. Even before the street violence started to escalate, I was always armed when I worked hookers. I carried my gun in a small purse with a shoulder strap, and when I was talking to a trick, I was always ready to pull on him. I seldom had to use my gun under those circumstances, but I would never have gone out on those streets unarmed.

I've seen just about everything on the street. One night a guy was shot while I was working undercover—he was driving a convertible, and somebody took a shot at him from the third floor—and the bullet whizzed right past my head. Apparently it was some kind of drug deal that went bad. The guy in the convertible, a drug addict, owed the guy with the gun, a drug dealer, some money and was refusing to pay up.

The hookers themselves have changed a lot over the years. You can forget your "hooker with a heart of gold" stereotype, Shirley MacLaine playing Irma la Douce. There's nothing *douce* about today's hookers. For the most part they're teenage runaways—uneducated, dirt-poor, abused kids with no feeling of self-worth whatsoever. There's nothing worldly-wise or sophisticated about them, no matter what movies and television would have you believe. Around here we get parents who push their daughters out on the street when they're twelve or thirteen years old.

Many of them are Mexicans who come here illegally. When the man of the house can't find work, he sits out on the steps drinking beer and sends his wife out to clean people's houses and his daughter out onto the streets to turn tricks. *Pretty Woman* it ain't.

The johns haven't changed too much over the years—they've always run the gamut from cute, sweet-faced, corn-fed virgins to the scariest lowlifes you can dream up, and they probably always will—but their special requests have. In the beginning they mostly wanted straight sex or maybe a head job, but the menu has become a lot more exotic with the passage of time. A few years ago I had an offer I'll remember for a while. Two guys drove up in a Toyota pickup. They were young and innocent-looking, as if they'd come straight from a Kansas cornfield. After they pulled up beside me, they told me what they had in mind. First they wanted me to give them both head jobs. Then one of them would have straight sex with me, and the other wanted anal sex. Then they'd like me to come to their hotel and watch a *video* of them having sex with each other. How much would all of that cost them, please? I realized they probably didn't come straight from Auntie Em's backyard after all.

This may sound strange, but the biggest, most significant change in the business of working hookers over the last twenty years is in the paperwork. The computer has changed everything, and it has definitely made a cop's life a lot easier. Under today's system a secretary sits in a van on the site, listens in on the cop-hooker's wire, and takes it all down. There's a standard arrest report set up on the computer screen, so all she has to do is fill in the blanks—

name of the suspect, details of the arrest—license number, physical description, and so forth—and the elements once the undercover cop has them. Then she prints out the report on the spot, and all the arresting officer has to do is sign it and go back to work. Before the dawning of the age of technology we'd have to cope with all that paperwork by hand; the process took ten times as long. Naturally, that meant that there were many fewer arrests. After we got the computers, I could arrest five guys in a row without missing a beat.

Not every encounter ended in an arrest. Sometimes the john would take off without giving me the elements. And once in a while I'd let somebody go, for reasons that wouldn't exactly stand up in a court of law.

Once, an employee of the telephone company stopped to do some business with me, in his official phone company truck, no less. Just as I was about to get the elements from him, I chanced to glance in his backseat and saw that it was full of all kinds of telephone equipment. I was sure that the stuff wasn't stolen, but I was also sure that if we arrested the guy, we'd have to account for everything in his truck. That is, *I* would have to account for everything in his truck. The moment I looked in the backseat, I had a crystal-clear picture of me labeling every one of those damn phones. With nightmarish visions of paperwork, I decided to kick him loose.

I couldn't just let him go, of course, so I scared him away, intimidated him so much that he never gave me the elements.

"Hi," he said after I had finished looking in his backseat.

He was very innocent-looking and was blushing profusely.

"I don't want no phone, man," I snarled back.

"Are you working?" he asked.

"Yes," I answered, without offering any encouragement.

"How much?"

He wouldn't take the hint. I decided to play hardball.

"Why do you wanna do this?" I said. "Why don't you just fuck off and get outta my way. You don't have enough money anyhow."

The guy took off like a shot, shouting, "Fuck you, bitch!" So much for a sweet face.

I looked up at my partner, Gary, this big crazy guy I loved to work with, because of his broad smile and his off-the-wall sense of humor. (Every time I arrested some-body he would crack up laughing; he also used to take pictures of me out on the street and give them funny cap-tions.) He had borrowed a truck and some coveralls and had positioned himself up on top of the power line next to me, pretending to do repairs. He was listening in on my wire, but he had absolutely no idea why I'd elected to blow a perfectly good bust. Of course, he hadn't seen all those phones.

Then there was Mr. Wonderful. I was working hookers on Ventura Boulevard, an upscale part of town, much ritzier than my usual division in Van Nuys. I had been loaned out for a few weeks to help with a special detail. It was a smog-free day, and I was in a good mood. A car pulled up, a big white convertible, and when I looked inside, I saw the most gorgeous hunk I had ever laid eyes on.

He stopped the car, stared through me with his chestnut-brown eyes, and said, "What would you like to be doing at this moment?"

This was a new one on me. I purred, "Well, I sure am tired of standing out here in the sun."

He smiled and said, "You shouldn't have to stand here. You should be someplace else, someplace wonderful. I want to give you this money."

Again, I hadn't heard that approach before. "You're gonna just *give* me this money?" I asked, watching him move his massive shoulders under his silk shirt.

He said, "Yes, I want to give you this money." He had three hundred-dollar bills in his hand, which he passed over to me. His hand lingered on mine.

"What do you want me to do for this money?" I stammered.

"I want you to meet me at my hotel at five o'clock," he said softly. "I would like you to do, and be, whatever you want. We'll just play it by ear. I just want to be alone with you."

Okay, I admit it—I was hypnotized by the guy. So I gave him back his money and kicked him loose. I'm a little surprised I didn't run off and marry him.

The guys in the van went *crazy*. They had heard every word, so they knew I had absolutely no reason to let the guy go. They accused me of being prejudiced and of thinking with some part of my anatomy other than my brains. It was weeks before they let it go. I had no defense for my "unprofessional behavior," so all I could do was sit back and take it. But somehow I didn't mind. The fantasy was worth it.

THERE ARE SOME johns I enjoyed arresting a lot more than others. I would occasionally feel sorry for the shy, scared kids, but I never felt an ounce of sympathy for the aggressive types who thought they were God's gift to hookers.

"Hey, baby, whadya got tonight that I haven't seen before?"

"Hey, you're new, aren't you, baby? You're not as old and ugly as some of 'em."

When you hear those kinds of things, you know you're dealing with a regular, and a real jerk at that. I *loved* nailing and arresting those guys.

I know that I make all this sound kind of fun, and that's because that's mostly what I remember. But I also remember many nights when I felt numbed by the experience. There were so many assholes! How could hookers even tell these jokers apart? They all seemed cloned from the same bad seed.

A few years on the Trick Task Force can teach a person a lot about human nature. It didn't take me long to develop a sixth sense about the johns who came my way. I think the scariest trick I ever came across was a big guy I called "Jean-Claude Killy." He pulled up in a big black sedan, and he wouldn't look at me. He just looked straight ahead and talked in a really low voice, like something out of a cheap horror movie. I never saw anyone so intense. I was having a lot of trouble getting the elements from him, and I began to realize that he was checking *me* out, looking for something in particular. I had seen serial sex crime suspects in the jail, and I knew that men who were into that always needed something specific to trigger their violence. There was nothing sexual about their crimes. They were into power. This guy was starting to give me the chills.

Then, right in the middle of our bizarre conversation, I glanced quickly at his backseat and saw a ski mask. The problem was, it wasn't ski season, and he didn't look like an athlete. With a tight grip on my gun, I eventually got the elements from him and the black-and-white took him away, after collecting a few other interesting items from the backseat: a camera, a pair of leather gloves, and a bottle of ether.

I've always had a warm spot in my heart for hookers—probably because I got to know them so well in the jail—but I'm not that crazy about johns. And I *hate* pimps. I hate their clothes, their cars, and their oily voices. Most of all I hate what they do to hookers. What a lot of people don't realize is that prostitution hasn't really got much to do with sex. For pimps and johns alike the appeal is power over women. Sick guys get off on controlling women and exploiting their ability and power to do so. There might be some "good" pimps in the world, but I sure never met any. The ones I came across seemed to enjoy hurting hookers. I used to think that most of them weren't in that business for the money at all; what they liked was inflicting pain. I could hardly believe what some of these animals did to those women.

Their favorite ploy was to get the whores hooked on drugs. They'd start some twelve-year-old girl (usually a runaway thinking she'd been "discovered") off on wine, doll her up, then send her out on the street to sell her body. Eventually they'd let the kid graduate from booze to hard drugs. Drugs are perfect for a pimp's purposes. They keep a hooker skinny and let her work long hours. And when a hooker becomes an addict, she doesn't have to be paid in cash. She'll work for her daily ration of crack or heroin.

Working pimps is a lot harder than working tricks; most pimps today are too smart—if that's the right word—to come after a hooker, or at least a cop posing as a hooker. They make us come to them. When I first started, a pimp would see me working his area and he'd walk right over, start moving in. Now they're suspicious, worried that behind every hooker there could be a cop, so that almost never happens anymore.

Getting the elements from a pimp can be a real pain, so much so that I often wondered if it was worth the trouble. Then I'd remember how much I hated those sleazebags and redouble my efforts. Before I could arrest a pimp when I was working hookers, he had to say, in so many words, that he wanted me to work for him, what my job description would entail, and how much money he was going to pay me to do it. A whole business conversation had to take place, specifically with me and about me. It wasn't enough to overhear him talking about money with another hooker or to find a hooker willing to testify about the pimp's business arrangement with her. He had to do business with *me*.

One of the scariest encounters I ever had with a pimp took place just a few years ago, during what was supposed to be a routine night on the Trick Task Force. Sergeant Lark was out with me, and just as we reached the site and were getting ready to move into position, something big went down in another part of the division. "Officer needs assistance," somebody said on the radio, and the van took off like a shot, with my partner in it. A few seconds later the black-and-white left too, and I was standing there on the street, alone. They had forgotten all about me.

I don't think I've ever felt more vulnerable than I did on that street corner that night. All of a sudden I wasn't a well-trained, experienced policewoman out on a detail. I was just Gayleen, stranded out there in the middle of Sepulveda Boulevard in the middle of the night, dressed like a hooker. In short, I was temporarily out of "character," and if I wasn't careful, I was about to be out of luck.

Naturally, one of the meanest-looking pimps I've ever seen was directly across the street from me, and he was watching my every move. That's what pimps usually do, stake out their prey, the way a shark circles a scuba diver. They check you out for a while, and then they come over for a little talk. That's what this pimp did. After looking me over for a few minutes, he slowly walked up to me.

I stood my ground as he approached. I knew that if I left, the patrol car would never find me. I didn't have a radio, because I was undercover, and I hadn't put my wire on yet. I also knew that if I didn't stop being plain old Gayleen and get back into character in a hurry, I was doomed.

"Hey, baby, what's shakin'?" the pimp said to me.

"Jus' workin'," I answered, trying desperately to sound as mean as he did.

"Oh yeah? Who you workin' for?" He moved closer.

"Nobody you know." I was starting to get my courage back.

"So, how much are you?" Now he was right up in my face.

"Listen, you don't have to think about it 'cause I'm goin' back to Hollywood."

He kept at me. "How long you been workin'?"

"Long enough," I said. "But maybe I'd like it here. Talk to me." Finally I stopped being myself and started kicking into character. My voice got harder, and I got meaner. I knew I was going to be okay.

Finally, my backup team returned. By then I had the elements I needed. I gave them time to get into position, then took off my hat—the signal for them to move in. Everybody jumped out and descended on the pimp at once. As he was cuffed, he turned to me and said, "Watch yourself, lady cop, you could get real hurt."

"Wait in line, pal," I answered.

After that, I took myself off the hooker detail for a few months. Those few moments of vulnerability—when I realized as I never had before that if anybody made a mistake out there, I could get myself hurt or even killed—left me more shaken than I had been in years and more nervous about my ability to bounce back. I wasn't sure my adrenaline pump was up to this shit. And I was in no hurry to get back out there anytime soon.

As word got around that I had a flair for working hookers, I was asked to train some of the other women. Fresh out of the Police Academy, most female police officers didn't picture themselves walking Sepulveda Boulevard in jeans and tight sweaters, talking to strangers about sex. They wanted to do Real Police Work—write traffic tickets, arrest criminals, that sort of thing. It was my job to show them that the Trick Task Force was Real Police Work, and they could sink their teeth into it.

The first step was to show them how to get the job done, starting from the beginning and going right on through to the signing of the arrest report. I taught them how to dress, how to talk, and—most important of all—how to act as if they belonged out there. I made them understand that they had to behave as if they *owned* the street. That's what I meant by being in character.

I would take them on a tour of the streets and point out significant things about the hookers—what they wear, how they stand, and so on. Then I'd give them a Berlitz course on some of the language they were going to be hearing, especially the code words for different kinds of sex acts— straight lay, head job, "50-50," golden shower—and the kind of street talk that real street people can immediately recognize. Then they were ready to watch me work for a couple of hours, sitting in the van and listening in on the wire. One of their assignments was to write down what I said and memorize some of the phrases.

When they felt ready, it was time for a test run. We'd work in pairs at first, so that with me next to them they could get comfortable with the johns and at the same time be protected. One girl I was training started to get into the car with a john, thinking she'd ride with him to the hotel. I caught her just in time. "Honey, don't get into that car unless you see his cash," I told her and pulled her out. I took over and talked the john into going to the hotel. We found a gun in his pocket. The only way to learn this job was hands on, with a safety net.

It didn't take long for the women, the good ones at least, to develop styles all their own. I always thought that training women for the Trick Task Force was as important for me as it was for them. It kept me sharp and reminded me, in case I needed it, of just how serious our business was on the street.

I loved working hookers—the crazy hours, the overtime, the unpredictability, even the danger. I liked being out on the street and working with the guys in Vice. And I truly *loved* putting assholes in jail, especially pimps. Still, I could never have done it full-time; it would have taken too much out of me. A few days or weeks here and there were terrific, but any more than that would have been too much of a good thing.

MY MOTHER WAS always very proud of her daughter the cop, but I always had the impression that my grandmother didn't really approve of my work, which isn't so strange when you consider that back in the twenties she made *her* living as a madam in one of the finest houses of prostitution in Hoquiam, Washington. I represented the enemy to her, although she'd never admit to her colorful past. She always insisted to me that she was completely legit. However, my mother still enthralls me with stories of her childhood adventures as the daughter of a madam and a bootlegger—such as the time Grandma, rather excitedly, told her to hide some bottles of moonshine Grandma happened to have around the house. Someone had tipped her off that she was about to be raided. Little La Verne (Mom's real name) did as she was told, carefully taking all the bottles outside and hiding them in the snow along the edges of the sidewalk. She stuck the last one in just as the cops marched up the walk, patting her on her head as they passed by on their way to do their righteous deed. Everything was great until the sun popped out for a rare visit and the snow started to melt. Mom ran frantically down the street, chasing the floating bottles and stuffing them in her wagon. As the cops came back out the front door, my quick-thinking mom yelled, "Do you want to see me dance?" "Sure, kid," the cops answered. (How could they turn down such a sweet little kid? So Mom proceeded to dance and dazzle the guys on their way back to their cars. They never noticed the wagon load of moonshine right in front of their eyes.

A few years before my grandmother died (she was a century baby, born New Year's Eve, 1900), my mother and I flew up to visit her in her new home in Milwaukie, Oregon. After we'd had a few glasses of wine, my tongue got a little loose, and I started relating some of my undercover adventures. I felt encouraged to keep on going when my mother started laughing in the middle of my story about the sixty-year-old banker who wanted to tie me up and dress himself in my clothes. I was so engrossed in my stories that I never noticed that one member of my audience, Grandma, was becoming increasingly silent. Finally, as I was describing the time I answered a newspaper ad for a masseuse and discovered the couple wanted to pay me to teach the wife how to give a great blow job, Grandma cleared her throat. Thinking that her red face was a decent indicator that I had gone too far, I shut up. I watched her take a sip of wine, and figured I was about to get a lecture on good manners. Instead, keeping her eyes focused on her glass, she asked me in a low voice, "I've been wondering, how much do they charge for what you call a 'blow job' these days?"

"Well, Grandma," I said, clearing *my* throat, "A straight blow job with no fancy extras goes for a street price of about twenty-five dollars."

With that, Grandma stood straight up out of her chair, knocking over her glass, and shouted, "Twenty-five dollars! If one of *my* customers had come into my place and only wanted to pay twenty-five dollars for some strange stuff like that, I'd have thrown him right down the stairs!"

I didn't dare sneak a glance at Mom. We both watched Grandma for a few seconds—her face struggling for control as she realized she had definitely let the cat out of the bag. Then she muttered something about having left the oven on, and marched out of the room. My mother managed to whisper to me before we joined her, "They only did straight lays in her day?" "I guess so!" I answered. That's one subject I never had the courage to bring up again.

FAMILY FEUDS

It is the policy of this Department that domestic violence is alleged criminal conduct and that a request for assistance in a situation involving domestic violence is the same as any other request for assistance where violence has occurred.

—FROM THE 1989 LAPD FIELD MANUAL
(RULE 240.20)

There are two things in police work that I really hate. One is having somebody—especially a little old lady with a pained expression—walk into the station carrying a big paper sack. (The wet ones are the worst.) And the other is getting a call about a "domestic disturbance." My reasons are the same in both instances: I never know what the hell I'm going to find when I look inside, but there's a better than even chance I'm not going to like it.

I read somewhere that every six hours in this country a woman is killed by her husband or boyfriend. I don't know what the statistics are for the city of Los Angeles, but what I do know is that for the twenty years I was on the force, there was always more than enough domestic violence to go around. Anytime I worked the night shift, I could count on having to stop at least one family argument.

In the time I spent on the job, there were two important changes in the area of domestic disputes. One has to do with the families themselves, and the other concerns how the police handle complaints of family violence.

Los Angeles has a heavily transient population, with a large number of immigrants from around the world, and over the years that influx of foreigners has made for a significant increase in family violence. I don't mean to suggest that wife-beating and other domestic disputes aren't as American as baseball and apple pie; there have always been and will always be dysfunctional families among those born in the USA. But family abuse is not normally shrugged off or even condoned in this country the way it is in some other cultures.

There are people living in Los Angeles today who moved here from countries in which women are regarded as men's property, to whom they can do whatever they like. When these families get to America, they see nothing wrong with continuing the old ways of their native lands. I once got a call from a man, a recent immigrant to this country, who wanted us to arrest his wife for leaving him. He had been beating her nearly senseless for quite some time—we knew that, because we had been called by her neighbors and had arrested the guy twice—but he was convinced that it was her duty to stay with the family. He couldn't believe that she had the right to walk out.

As long as there have been police officers, there have been late-night calls about disturbances in the apartment upstairs or the house next door. In the old days we would answer the call, check out what was happening, and use our discretion to solve the problem. Sometimes that meant intervention, sitting a man and a woman down and helping them work out their problems—after we took the rolling pin and the broom away from them. (Cops are trained in psychology and given special courses in counseling battered women and coping with family disputes.) Other times it meant taking one or even both of them off to jail. When the system worked the way it was supposed to, we would calm the family down and leave them in peace. We used our instincts and experience to evaluate each situation.

Today it's all handled differently. According to department regulations that were put into effect in 1987, if a man hits his wife today, a police officer called to the scene has no choice but to take the offender to jail immediately and book him on a felony charge of spousal abuse. Even if no one in the house wants anyone to be arrested, even if we think it's the wrong thing to do—and often we do think so—we have to make that arrest.

The thinking behind that all-important policy change was the belief that the threat of an arrest serves as a deterrent to people prone to domestic violence. The lawmakers got fed up with having officers called to the same address night after night, with the same result: tears, apologies, heartfelt promises never to do it again, and then a repeat performance the next evening. They figured that if the Battling Bickersons knew they were going to go to jail, they'd stop battling and get their act together.

There are two problems with this theory: one, it hasn't worked; there are just as many calls about domestic violence as ever. And two, the arrests don't stick anyway. More than nine out of ten of the people we take in manage to plea-bargain their way back home in a couple of days, usually madder and meaner than before.

The change in the law hasn't made cops' lives any easier, and I'm not even sure that in the long run it has made the problem any less severe. I know that many of us had to act against our better judgment, carting people off to jail instead of helping them work out what they were fighting about in the first place. Still, there is one definite advantage to doing things the new way. When I see a bruised and battered woman who is obviously too terrified and brow-beaten to lodge an official complaint against her husband, I'm glad that the decision is no longer in her hands. If *I* see bruises or cuts, *I* can file a complaint and take the guy away.

On the other hand, there are plenty of times I had to make a report when I didn't think that the interests of justice were going to be served if I did. One night, for instance, we got a call from a woman who said that her neighbors seemed intent on killing each other. The noise coming from next door was unbelievable—crashing, bang-ing, all kinds of mayhem—and it had been going on for hours.

When we responded to the call, it looked as if a bomb had gone off in the apartment. To my surprise, the man and woman responsible for the wreckage were unscathed. When they got mad, they said, they didn't believe in hitting each other. ("Why would I hit her?" the husband said. "I love her." "I love him, too," said his wife.) They believed that the way to solve their problems was to bust up the place.

The wife took charge of the kitchen. First she broke the plates and glassware; then she started in on the groceries. There were pieces of broken crockery and mounds of corn flakes and oatmeal all over the room. The living room was obviously the husband's domain. Just as methodical as his spouse, he had picked up every piece of furniture in the room and thrown it against the far wall. When we arrived on the scene, the couple appeared to be winding down. They seemed almost cheerful.

There were a couple of kids in the house, but they were in their room, watching television with the sound turned way up. They looked like something right out of *Ozzie and Harriet*. The scene couldn't have been more tranquil.

"Are you guys all right?" I asked them when I could tear them away from their TV program.

"We're fine," one of them replied cheerfully. "Mommy and Daddy are just fighting."

To tell you the truth, the whole crazy scene struck my partner and me as funny, but our hands were tied. Mommy and Daddy both had bruises on their arms and had to be arrested, and those cheerful kids were going to have to spend at least a few nights in a foster home.

I'm not sure exactly when we stopped saying "wife-beat-ing" and started calling it "spousal abuse." I suppose it happened when the number of complaints from men claim-ing to have been battered by their wives began to increase. When a cop shows up at the scene of a domestic dispute, it's not at all unusual to have each party accuse the other of being abusive. If it looks as if both of them have been injured, we can't discriminate. We take them both in.

Normally we're faced with situations that are pretty unambiguous, but occasionally, the chore of figuring out who is doing what to whom is a lot more complicated than it may seem. For instance, imagine that a husband and wife have a big fight, and my partner and I are called to the scene. When we get there, each of the two principals starts accusing the other of bloody murder. Both have scratches and bruises on their faces and arms. What's going on here?

"He beat me up!" shrieks the wife.

"She beat *me* up!" countershrieks the husband.

"Yes, but he beat *me* up first. I was just protecting myself!" she fires back.

It's only the aggressor we want to arrest, and with luck a witness will be able to help us choose one. If not, we have to take them both in.

Sometimes the scene of a domestic battle is all too clear. One of the saddest sights I ever saw was one rainy night about seven years ago when I had to check out a young couple on welfare who were arrested for fighting almost every Friday night. Again, a neighbor had called in to com-plain about the noise. When my partner and I got there, one of the kids answered the door.

"Mommy and Daddy are killing each other," the little girl cried, gesturing to the back bedroom where the commotion was. Sure enough, both her parents had knives and looked as if they were planning to use them. Behind her, in the small, cluttered living room, her brother and sister were cowering in fear. That wasn't the first time I noticed that family violence is terrifying to children. I once saw a four-year-old child punching his little sister while his parents slugged it out in the next room. School for future abusers was in session.

Strictly speaking, the crime of "spousal abuse" doesn't apply only to husbands and wives. It can cover a multitude of other relationships, including boyfriends and girlfriends and gay relationships, both male and female. Over the years we got quite a few calls about people who were abusing their elderly parents. We'd answer a call from a concerned neighbor and find out that some forty-year-old "child" was regularly beating one or both of his parents. Sometimes the motive was that the kid wanted to get rid of the old folks to collect on their life insurance. More often, though, what was happening was simply the most recent installment of a grotesque family drama. Having been abused as children, the younger generation was retaliating against the parents, treating them exactly as they had been treated when they were little.

To interfere in the affairs of a family in chaos can be dangerous business, and the police officer who does so needs any edge he can muster. I've always thought that the most important thing I could have in a family dispute is a good, reliable partner, someone who is quick to see what's wrong equally quick to cool it down, to make it right. I've had several really good partners, and each of them taught me a different way to approach this job.

The first thing we did when we showed up at the scene was to separate the two people who were fighting. Under most circumstances, I would take the man into another room, and my partner—usually a male—would stay and talk to the woman. Normally there wouldn't be any problem if I interviewed the woman (sometimes it even worked better), but if the two men paired up, sparks were more than likely to fly. The husband, still heated from the fight with his wife, often lost his temper and came on too strong with my male partner.

We had two goals: one, to establish the facts, and two, to calm everyone down, not stir things up. Being female, I had a better chance than my partner of being able to cool an irate husband down to room temperature.

What nearly always worked was sympathy.

"I'm looking at the pictures on the wall and I see how much you love your wife," I would usually begin, making him think I was a hundred percent on his side. "I know you really didn't mean to hurt her when you threw that knife." It wouldn't take long for him to tell me his side of the story. Meanwhile, my partner would be operating the woman in the other room, sympathizing with her and getting on her good side. His approach was much the same as mine: "I know you have a real problem with your husband. Why don't you tell me what happened." Then the floodgates would open, and he'd try to look interested in her story— one he'd heard at least a hundred times before.

If everything went according to schedule, we would eventually calm them down, at least enough so that they were harmless, if not completely rational. Then we'd put one or both of them in jail.

Being able to tell when someone is telling the truth is one of the most important skills a cop can develop. Lie detectors would be tremendously helpful, but only if the guilty would consent to use them. But anytime you have to deal with human nature, there's not a gadget anywhere that can hold a candle to the instincts of a good cop. Nothing can or will ever take the place of a good, old-fashioned hunch.

I've always believed in playing my hunches, but never more than when I interrogated witnesses and suspects. Over the years I've had my share of success interrogating difficult cases, the ones no one else wanted anything to do with. A few years ago nearly everybody in the division was talking about the confession I managed to pry out of a poor, troubled girl who had made a false accusation. She was only fifteen years old—technically a minor—and had filed a complaint against two young officers who had arrested her for shoplifting. She claimed they had forced her to give them head jobs in the backseat of their black-and-white before taking her into the station. Their supervisor, Lieutenant Don Kitchen, asked me to check out her story. We drove over to her house. She ignored Don as she sat on the couch and toyed with her hair, talking in a scattered way about how men are so scary. We spent most of the time chatting about how frustrating men are; I pretended I was a single woman and completely on her side. She finally confessed that her story wasn't true. She was simply mad at the officers because they had arrested her in front of her friends. My lieutenant was saved from days of painful investigation and interviews. (Each complaint against an officer requires a supervisor to spend a hell of a lot of time trying to determine if there's been real misconduct on the part of the officer.) Case closed. In my next Rating Report I was commended for my "outstanding interrogation techniques."

People have always felt comfortable telling me things. I think it's because I try so hard to identify with the point of view of the person I'm interrogating. Whatever my personal feelings are, I do anything I can to make the person feel comfortable with me. Sometimes it means making him understand that we have a lot in common. Other times I just stress the fact that I understand how he feels, even if I'm trying to get him to confess to something unspeakable.

"You must have been really angry," I might say, or "I can really understand why you did it." One of my cardinal rules was never to ask a suspect *if* he did it. I always told him I understood *why* he did it. Even bad guys need to feel positive about themselves before they can let down their guard and start communicating.

On occasion I'd play good cop, sympathizing with the suspect about how he was being treated by the police. "I know it's really hard to be arrested," I might tell him. "Handcuffs are really terrible." The real skill is in knowing which tack to take.

There's one other important thing that makes me good with people in trouble: I understand and appreciate what it's like to be victimized. It's frustrating and horribly difficult to be a victim, and very common for victims to become angry at the person who's most convenient, even if that person has been hired by the city to protect and serve them. If some poor man has worked for months to buy his child a bicycle and then that bicycle is stolen when it's only a few hours old, he gets incensed, and I can understand why. If another guy gets mugged or has his car stolen, he can lose control and lash out. Rape victims are especially prone to take out their anguish on a police officer, especially a male. All of these reactions are completely understandable to me.

One of the most wrenching experiences I ever had with an angry victim was when I had to comfort a man who had just learned that his daughter and son-in-law had been found dead in their home. He was devastated by the news itself, but he was channeling his distress into anger at the way the police department was handling the investigation. When he came into the station, he was out for *blood*, LAPD blood. The sergeant asked me to calm him down.

I put my arm around the man's shoulders and said, very softly, "I know how mad you must be. You've had some devastating news. You must have loved your daughter very much. I know I love mine."

He started crying first, choking the sobs out in painful bursts. I held him in my arms and rocked him like a child. Gradually, I got him to understand and accept that the deaths of his daughter and son-in-law weren't really the department's fault. Taking his frustrations out on us cops wouldn't make him feel any better. A few days later the man sent me a dozen red roses with a card saying how much he appreciated my patience and compassion. Cops aren't allowed to accept gratuities, but I decided to make an exception. In fact, I wore a rose on my uniform for inspection that day.

No DISCUSSION OF family problems would be complete without talking about runaways. Back when I first came on the job, it was a big deal when a teenager ran away from home. Everybody in the neighborhood would be out ringing doorbells and looking for the kid. When the kid was found—as he usually was—he would be in big trouble, not only with his parents but with the law. The incident went on the kid's record, and he often had to spend time in Juvenile Hall, something no kid in his right mind wanted to do. You see, in those days it was actually against the law for a child to be a runaway. Today it's practically a national sport. When the law changed, in 1980, the party line was that running away from home was being decriminalized because it was, after all, the responsibility of the parents, not the courts, to look after the welfare of children. The truth is, tracking down runaways was just getting too expensive; sending a truckload of police out to look for teenagers simply cost too much time and money. Besides, Juvenile Hall was getting filled up. The first ten years I was on the force I saw only a trickle of runaway reports, but in the late seventies that trickle started to become a tidal wave.

Once virtually nobody was looking for them anymore, runaway kids found it a lot easier to live on the streets—

easier, that is, once they discovered the economic benefits of prostitution or selling drugs or the art of picking pockets. I have a friend who's a real expert on runaways. After he retired from the police force, he got a job working security in the Greyhound bus station. (Crime is so bad in the Los Angeles Greyhound station that the bus company hired two off-duty police officers to walk a beat in there twenty-four hours a day.) One day he started talking about what he'd learned.

"You can always spot a runaway in the bus station because he's walking around with a shopping bag," he began. "A runaway kid is not going to swipe his momma's best luggage. He's going to grab a bag, throw some clothes in it, and take off. When the folks go off to work, he'll pretend to go to school, and that will give him a solid eight hours before they know he's missing. So he jumps on a bus and comes here. By the time we get them, they're tired, hungry, and maybe a little desperate."

Of course, spotting runaways doesn't necessarily do anyone much good, least of all the kid. As my friend explains it, "We pick them up, but we can't hold them. We have no authority over runaways. Running away isn't a crime, so we can't put them in Juvenile Hall. We always try to call the parents, and sometimes they'll come for them, and Greyhound tries to help by volunteering to give them a free bus ticket home. But if they don't want to listen to us, they can walk out the door, right into God knows what. Once a week I talk to a thirteen- or fourteen-year-old who's in tears because some guy has taken him into a hotel room and turned him into an adult before he was ready."

THERE ISN'T A cop alive who isn't haunted by some story of what might have been. One of my stories has to do with a spousal abuse case gone wrong.

The guys on the desk got a call from a woman who sounded desperate. She was having trouble with her live-in boyfriend, and she needed some police protection. "I'm in terrible trouble," she said. "I need to talk to a woman about it." The case was turned over to me, and I asked her to come to the station right away.

I'll never forget the first time I saw that woman. Black, beautiful, impeccably dressed, she had people stopping in their tracks as she walked through the station to my desk. She was an interior designer, she said. She'd been divorced for a few years and had been dating several men during that time. For the last few months she had been seeing just one man, but a couple of weeks earlier she had broken their relationship off. The guy had started to make her uneasy, she explained. He was insanely jealous and possessive, always demanding to know where and with whom she was going to be every minute of the day. She finally got fed up with his attitude and told him she didn't want to see him anymore.

That only made his behavior worse. Ever since the day she broke up with him, he had been following her everywhere, waiting outside her office while she worked and

sometimes taunting her from a few feet away. We couldn't
help her—neither of those acts were illegal. There were
obscene phone calls too, at all hours of the night, but she
couldn't prove they were from him. She had received a
couple of packages containing pornographic pictures, and
although once again she couldn't prove it, she was sure he
had given the company her address. She was certain that he
was responsible for everything. She moved and changed her
phone number, but he found her again. By the time I talked
to her, she was scared to death—and I didn't blame her one
goddamned bit.

I wanted to tell her to run like hell, to change her name
and leave town with no forwarding address, but I couldn't
do that. That wasn't part of my job. My job was to try to
make the system work for this poor woman. We would have
loved to arrest the guy, but we didn't have any grounds.
None. After all, he hadn't actually threatened her, and we
had zero proof that the packages and calls had come from
him. I advised her to get a restraining order forbidding him
to come anywhere near her. I told her to keep in touch and
call if he tried anything else. Two weeks later the call came
through: shots had been fired at that lovely woman's new
apartment. She was dead.

I can't tell you how many times I've reproached myself for
that woman's death. I still feel guilty about it. But the terrible
fact of the matter is that I did everything I could under the law
to protect her. As much as I might have wanted to put that
asshole in jail—or, better yet, shoot him between the eyes—
and as much as you might think that's what I should have

done, that kind of thing just happens on TV cop shows. On television, police officers commit more felony violations— beating people up, pushing them around, intimidating them—in ten minutes than I saw in all my years on the force. Our job is to make sure the letter of the law is followed—and to do that we've got to follow it ourselves. Is it frustrating? Shit, yes. Is it necessary? The answer's the same.

There are times every police officer does battle with his conscience. None of us was ever happy with the idea that we couldn't stop an irate boyfriend from gunning down a nice, beautiful interior designer. But we had to work with and within the system. When the rules changed, even when we felt citizens were left unprotected, we had to act objectively. I made life and death decisions, not based on my opinion but based on the law and on departmental policy. Often those decisions were made in a matter of seconds.

Police officers aren't judges, and they aren't juries. That was a hard-to-take truth I had to embrace. Another was that it was not my responsibility to change the world. All I had to do—all I *could* do—was do my job. The Field Manual expresses it rather coldly, as usual; it says that police officers are charged with "the responsibility of the investigation, the apprehension, and the beginning of the process for the adjudication of the offense." Roughly translated, that means we're supposed to try to arrest the bad guys. What happens after that is up to somebody else. It's not a police officer's job to decide whether someone's guilty or innocent. It *is* a cop's job to evaluate what he sees, to listen carefully to what he's told, and to do his best to determine whether or not a crime has been committed—and, if so, by whom.

When I interviewed a victim, my job was to find out every single reason that victim felt a crime had been committed. When I wrote my report, it was my job to put all that down on paper so it made sense. Above all else, it was my job to get at the truth. If a suspect had an alibi or even an explanation, I had to check it out. If a suspect says, "I couldn't have done it because I was with my girlfriend and my mother and father and we were having dinner at seven o'clock tonight— that witness is lying," the detectives can't just take the witness's word and throw the guy in jail. Cops work for the defense as well as the prosecution. Cops have to investigate further, making enough inquiries to substantiate whether or not what the suspect is saying is true. Then, no matter what they discover, it all goes down in the report.

The system is not perfect. That's for damn sure. I've seen people convicted who in my opinion weren't guilty, and I've seen people who were guilty as sin walk free because of a legal technicality. (The only way I lasted twenty years was to try as hard as I could not to let it become my problem. I once thought of having a sampler embroidered for my wall: *Cops shovel it, judges sort it, jails process it—and it still comes out garbage.*)

If I were ever to forget that fact, all I would have to do is call to mind a supposedly open-and-shut case of lewd conduct that a Vice cop friend of mine, Jerry, was involved in not too long ago. Some young hunk had grabbed Jerry by his balls during an undercover operation in Sepulveda Park, and he had two reliable witnesses who were able to swear to what happened. When the case went to trial, it turned out not to be so open and shut after all. They ended up with a hung jury, and the guy walked.

Why a hung jury when the evidence was ironclad and the arrest had gone like clockwork? Well, there were two elderly ladies on the jury who just couldn't *believe* that a man would walk up and grab another man in that way.

Believe me, there are times I really envy those two little old ladies.

MY LIFE UNDERCOVER

In order to obtain information and evidence regarding criminal activities, it may be necessary that the Department utilize undercover operators. Such operators shall not become "Agents Provocateurs" or engage in entrapment.

—FROM THE 1989 LAPD FIELD MANUAL
(RULE 546)

Women make the best undercover cops. I suspected as much when I joined the police force, and twenty years later, when I left, I hadn't seen anything that changed my mind. Don't get me wrong. I think men can do a great job too. I just believe that when it comes to seducing people and getting them to fall for a line of bullshit, there's no one better at it than a woman. No one is better than a woman at making a suspect feel comfortable enough to commit a crime.

In undercover police work we talk about "operating"

people. I doubt that Webster puts it quite this way, but operating somebody means placing yourself in the position of a victim in order to get the elements from a suspect. Most of the outstanding operators I met on the job were women. I know it was *my* specialty.

My fellow officers on the force might quibble about whether women are better than men at undercover work, but the fact is, they welcome the feminine touch. I worked undercover on and off for all of my years on the force, even during that first stint in the jail. Most often I worked hookers for the Trick Task Force, but I did other assignments for Vice too, including gambling. I also was loaned out to Narcotics and, once in a while, Homicide.

In 1967 and 1968, when my official assignment was the Van Nuys Jail, I was loaned out to Homicide quite often. I loved the guys in Homicide; they had the kind of crazy, off-the-wall, I've-seen-it-all sense of humor that I love, probably because they *had* seen it all. To them nothing was too outrageous or taboo, and I was stimulated and amused by their way of looking at the world.

They liked me, too, I think, because I was enthusiastic and didn't fall apart when I saw something gruesome, which in Homicide was just about a daily occurrence. The first time I worked on abortion detail I saw a dead fetus and didn't flinch. After that, the guys in Homicide used to call the jail and ask for me whenever they had something they thought could use a woman's touch. Naturally, I couldn't work Homicide permanently back then. Women weren't allowed.

The Homicide assignment I remember best was the abortion detail I worked in 1968. Abortion was illegal in California back then, and there was a flourishing illegal abortion business all over Los Angeles. Gypsies had the market nearly cornered, but many immigrant doctors, not licensed to practice medicine in the United States, were making a nice living at it as well. Women were desperate then. There were no legal, sanitary clinics to go to and no financial assistance for the poor. They did what they had to do, and they paid the price for it. Sometimes the price was a life, or the chance of ever having another pregnancy.

Illegal abortions become Homicide's problem when there was a death. They would usually hear about it from the dead girl's parents. (Most of the victims were poor teenage girls.) Once we found a sixteen-year-old girl's body in a dumpster. When we interrogated the girl's friends and family, everyone was quite secretive at first, but eventually one of her sisters broke down and told us about her abortion. Even more important, she gave us the doctor's name and address.

That's where I came in. I had just turned twenty-five, but I looked younger. With the right makeup and costume I could pass as a pregnant teenager. We knew that, because I had gone undercover to arrest abortionists before. My record was *very* good.

I knew the drill: my job was to get in to see Dr. X., find out what he was using to perform the abortion (the most common tool was a coat hanger with a special blade attached), and get the elements of the crime. That meant establishing that he was going to perform an abortion on me and how much he was going to charge. Ideally I would get him to describe exactly what instrument he was going to use and what it would do to me.

First I had to convince the doctor that I was indeed pregnant, or at least thought I was. (Most of the illegal abortionists didn't actually care if girls were pregnant, provided they got paid.) Then I let him incriminate himself.

I didn't think that operating abortionists were going to be easy or pleasant, but I was not prepared for the horrors I saw. I'd never seen such filth. In the offices I visited during that stint, there was dirt and blood everywhere. Sometimes aborted fetuses were stashed in metal coffee cans. Sometimes they were in soup bowls or trash bags. The smell of rotten human flesh was unbearable, and the "doctor" was usually just as vile.

That detail was the first gruesome assignment I had on the police force. It may also have been the most depressing assignment I ever had. But at least I knew my actions were saving other women. The day I went to see Dr. X, four minutes after I walked into that office he told me that he'd be happy to give me an abortion and that he'd be using a small wire. He even held it up so that I could see it. No, he wouldn't be using an anesthetic. The cost? Fifty dollars. The fucker was in jail three hours later.

I liked being assigned to cases other cops didn't want. I enjoyed my "mission impossible" status, although I knew it wasn't due to the fact that I was a better cop than the ones who'd tried and failed to get a job done. It was simply that I had my own peculiar way of tackling a problem. I specialized in being "dumb like a fox."

I remember getting a call from Vice about a bar on Van Nuys Boulevard that the department just couldn't get into, no matter what the hell they tried. We had received tons of complaints about the place—a semiprivate club, run by Iranians, that seemed to specialize in illegal gambling, watered-down booze, and maybe a lot of other illegal activities, including narcotics. The word was that they were charging some of their unsuspecting customers—mostly other Iranians—double to get into the place and then making them pay champagne prices for cheap, watered-down booze. We needed to get into the place to operate it, but the Vice guys couldn't get past the front door.

So they asked me to give it a try.

I figured subtlety wasn't going to get me anywhere in a place like that, so I pulled out all the stops when I put together my outfit for the evening. My black low-cut dress with a slit up the side left almost nothing to the imagination, and I frizzed my hair up into a big blond halo. Then I put on my highest heels and my longest earrings and I was ready for action. A feather boa draped over my shoulder drew attention away from my little purse, where I carried my gun. I wanted to look seductive and appealing but not like a hooker; the look I was striving for was of somebody who was out to have a good time. "I'm friendly, innocent, and helpless" is what I was trying to announce. That's my trademark undercover pose.

Very late one night I walked up to the door of the club— my partner hung back a few steps—and was greeted by an ominous-looking Iranian doorman. I went right into my dizzy blonde act. It never fails, and, believe me, it has saved my ass both on and off the job more times than I can count.

"Hi," I said brightly. "You know what? I'm supposed to meet this guy, he's really nice and kind of cute, but he's got this name I can't pronounce."

He didn't look very friendly yet. I pressed on.

"Maybe you know him. He's got black hair and brown eyes and this really long name." Now I was hanging all over the doorman, turning on the charm. He seemed to be weakening.

"Could you just go in there and ask if there's somebody waiting for Caroline? [I used my middle name when I operated somebody.] Or maybe I should just go in and look for him. What do you think?"

It worked. He told me to go on in, and I started through the door. Then, as if I had just remembered something, I looked back at my partner and said, "Oh, I'm supposed to bring him, too. We're all real good friends."

The doorman didn't like it, but he'd gone too far to turn back now. He let us both go in.

I stayed in character as I worked the room, looking for the elements. I ordered a drink; sure enough, it was half water. While I was at the bar, I made sure to notice whether any other laws were being broken—whether they were giving liquor to minors or serving drunks. We ordered dinner and kept watching as we ate. In those kinds of places most of the action takes place late at night to early morning, so we were planning to stay until the club closed. Our persistence paid off. By closing time my partner and I had enough evidence to convict them of gambling, prostitution, and selling watered-down liquor. It was a good night's work.

Going undercover to look for gambling gave me a chance to use some of what I had learned from my stepfather. He'd been a small-time bookie and he taught me about handicapping, odds, and the glamorous world of high-stakes poker. In L.A. you can find illegal gambling almost everywhere you look, from coffee shops and insurance companies to church social halls. In most cases the police left them alone, but whenever we had one of the "Three Cs,"—Conspicuous, Commercial, or Complaint—we had to move in and check it out.

On one of the operations I was assigned to, we went looking for gambling in a Greek restaurant over on Sepulveda Boulevard—the street that's the prostitute's and the drug dealer's home away from home. It wasn't Conspicuous, and we didn't know yet if it was Commercial, but we *had* gotten a Complaint, from a distraught woman who told us that her husband had gambled away their entire life savings and was getting ready to lose the house as well. One of the Three Cs was enough.

Again, I thought I would try to make a powerful first impression, so I showed up at the scene in a fire-engine red one-shoulder jumpsuit. I was the only blonde in the restaurant, so *I* was definitely Conspicuous even if the gambling wasn't. My date for the evening was one of my favorite guys from Vice, a quiet little guy who could think faster on his feet than practically anyone I'd ever worked with. The first thing I did when I got to the restaurant was to pretend to ditch my date, walk slowly over to the bar, and introduce myself to the bartender. He seemed happy to make my acquaintance.

The main part of the restaurant had tables and a small dance floor, with a jukebox right near the bar. There were several people having dinner, and a few couples were dancing. The place was halfway between crowded and empty, just the way my partner and I liked it. Neither of us thought that there was any gambling in the main room; we figured the tables had to be set up in a room out back. Now all we had to do was get there.

I worked the bartender for a while, and soon we were joined by the owner's son, who immediately started acting like a first-class jerk—showing off for me, talking about what an incredibly successful, virile guy he was, bragging how he really knew how to show a girl a good time. I couldn't have been happier. That macho braggart type is perfect when you're trying to get information; their mouths are always bigger than their brains (and are also usually bigger than another part of their anatomies). I played the jukebox and let him do the talking. He was practically tying himself in knots to impress me. Pretty soon he was hinting that if I wanted some real fun, he could take me somewhere. And it wasn't very far away at all. I knew I was just about there.

But things got a little complicated right about then, because I had attracted another admirer, a little guy who had fallen head over heels in lust with me. I must have been about five eleven in my spike heels—to his five four standing on tiptoe—but he didn't care. He was determined to make his move. I tried not to be rude to the guy (after all, he was just a regular customer who wanted his share of fun), but I had to get rid of him. He didn't take any of the subtle hints I gave him to get lost; he simply wouldn't leave me alone so that I could operate those people. I hated to do it, but I asked the owner's son to help me out.

The son was in heaven. Now he had a chance to show me what a real man he was. He bullied the little guy right out of the restaurant, maybe even out of the state. Then we were alone at last, my Greek god protector and I. I've met a lot of guys who were full of themselves, but this would-be Adonis was in a class by himself. He was dressed all in white—tight pants with no underwear underneath, transparent shirt that was half unbuttoned, gold jewelry that wouldn't quit. And he thought that he was *smooth*.

For another half hour I pretended he was wonderful, and he bought it, every word of it. Then, I struck gold—he asked me if I wanted to go where the action was.

"What about my date?" I asked him.

"*I'm* your date," he replied. Arresting him wasn't going to sting my conscience at all.

We went upstairs, and there it all was, just like in the movies: bright lights, champagne, and wall-to-wall gambling tables. At first glance I could see blackjack and poker. I took my time, working it for a couple of hours to make sure I had all the elements, including names of the people who were there (they'd be called as witnesses later). Halfway through I went to the ladies' room and took a few notes, drawing a detailed picture of the room and writing down some key facts. I didn't have a tape recorder; it would have been too dangerous. All I had in my purse was a gun.

I returned to the gambling tables and continued to scope out the place, still hanging on the owner's son's every word. He was being a big help, strutting around the room, pointing out anything he thought I might have missed, and introducing me to his important patrons. His father had taken the night off, and Junior was playing master of ceremonies to the hilt. My partner, who had left the restaurant and gone outside, was waiting for my signal. When I was satisfied that I had all the elements, I was to go over to the window and light a cigarette. After a couple of hours I signaled to him, and we closed the place down. All we had to do then was the paperwork.

Paperwork—that's when undercover work becomes tedious. Perhaps nightmarish is a better word.

After a night like the one I just described, everything I had seen and heard was evidence, and it was my job to get it all down in black and white. Eye witnesses had to be identified and a list of their names and addresses prepared. Statements had to be taken and transcribed. Evidence had to be gathered, categorized, and labeled. As a reward for a job well done, my partner and I got to do all that and more. Then we had to go to court.

Court is even worse than paperwork. I hated everything about going to court—giving my statements to the attorneys, keeping track of papers, being responsible for the evidence. Most of all I hated the sitting around and waiting to be called, more often than not for one continuance after another. I don't like to admit this, but there were times that it took so long for a case to go to trial that I had all but forgotten the details. I don't see how any cop can keep all that stuff in his or her mind. Of course, that's why that paper trail is so important. That's why reports have to be perfect.

The whole court experience can be pretty numbing, especially if a police officer specializes in one category of crime. If you work on forgery all day every day, for instance, all the cases start to sound alike after a while. On one night of working hookers sometimes there would be ten cars lined up with drivers waiting to be serviced in some way or another, and I'd end up arresting most of the drivers. In each case I'd have to remember exactly what was said. I could never have done it without my notes. I could barely manage it with them.

Much of my life as an undercover cop was spent somewhere on Van Nuys Boulevard. I'd be lying if I said I liked that street, but there is one thing I can say about it: when you're out there looking for crime, there's never a dull moment. Much of it is lined with apartment houses, and behind the apartments are dark alleys that are open invitations to any and all criminals in the area. The parking lots along the street come in handy as well. Most of the street action involves gangs, especially burglaries and stolen cars.

After a few years on Van Nuys I thought I had seen it all. Then, one night I was working Vice and we got a call to check out a possible dead guy in an X-rated motel. The place was one of the most popular sex motels on the strip, because it had a reputation of offering something for everyone. Or anything for anyone. If there was a sex act you could think of, that place could fulfill your dreams. There were waterbeds, mirrored ceilings, and X-rated movies. No big deal—all the motels in the area had those. But this place had an S-M room and hidden video cameras, too, so that guests could be immortalized during sex. Even the parking lot was special. When my partner, Ed, and I walked through it, we agreed that neither of us had ever seen so many people having sex in public before.

The dead man was in Room 8, yet another of the specialty rooms. As we discovered, his particular sexual pleasure involved electrical shocks to his genitals, and that's what had killed him. The motel management had provided the room, and he had hooked up a couple of wires to his penis and testicles. The idea was to give himself an orgasm with tiny shocks, but apparently he got carried away.

Later I learned from the coroner, who really *had* seen it all, that this sort of thing happened all the time. Lots of guys got their rocks off from electrical shocks, and the more they tried it, the more volts they needed to be satisfied. Many of them ended up just the way our guy in Room 8 did: death by electrocution.

Not all of my sordid undercover adventures took place in Los Angeles's less desirable neighborhoods. One thing I knew from my burlesque days was that the upper classes can get down and dirty just as easily as the guys living on Skid Row. The difference is, the guys with money are harder to get next to.

Some time in the early eighties we had a complaint about the activities taking place in one of those mansions up on the hill in Sherman Oaks, on Mulholland Drive. One of the neighbors complained that there was group sex going on in this big, beautiful house, and she was sure that all kinds of money was changing hands. And drugs, too, for all she knew. What's more, she said, she had seen a police helicopter cruising the area, watching the festivities, for several nights running. Why hadn't we blown the whistle on these people?

My partner, Don, and I were assigned to investigate. To do that we had to get into the house. We went as Mr. and Mrs. Russell—Dave and Susie—friendly neighbors who had recently moved into the area and just wanted to get acquainted. My partner wore white pants and a flowered shirt that had one too many buttons undone. I was in a kind of cabana outfit, tight and bright, and I topped it off with a big floppy straw hat. We wanted to look friendly and a little loose.

From the outside the house looked completely normal— no signs of anything kinky or illegal were visible from the front yard. When a woman answered the door, we were all smiles. I was at my dizziest.

"Oh, hi! We're Dave and Susie Russell, and we just moved into the neighborhood, and we just love it here, but we're a teeny bit bored, and we were hoping that you could tell us about something exciting to do around here and oh, you have *such* a beautiful home." I think I said the whole thing without taking a breath.

The woman invited Dave and me into the house—we didn't leave her much choice—and that's when we realized there was a party going on. There were about twenty people there, and even at first glance they looked friendlier than your average cocktail party guests. There was some heavy petting going on, and a couple of women were walking around topless.

"Ooh, a *party*!" I squealed. "Dave and I just *love* parties. Don't we, honey?"

"Dave" said yes, we did love parties.

"Please, why don't you have a drink and stay awhile?" the woman said to us. We had passed inspection.

Still in my dizzy blonde mode I wandered all over the house, admiring the furniture, the paintings, and the knick-knacks and introducing myself to everyone. The hostess's husband took to me right away. I could tell because he backed me into a corner and insisted I have a drink with him. We talked and drank for a while, and then I knew it was time to move on.

I said I had to go to the "little girls' room," and he pointed me in the right direction. As I was making my way there, some guy I hadn't even noticed grabbed me and pulled me into a dimly lit room. Right away I could tell he was drunk and stoned. We were all alone in the room, and he had me in a tight hold, breathing hard directly in my face.

"Don't you just love sex with animals?" he asked.

I have to confess: for once in my life I couldn't think of anything to say. I gave him a weak smile.

He continued. "I just love sex with animals. I fuck dogs. And I get 'em to lick my cock."

I still didn't answer him, but he couldn't have cared less.

He was perfectly content with his one-way conversation. He went on describing in great detail the deeply moving love affair he had been having with the animal kingdom. Meanwhile, he had me in an armlock and was pinning me against the wall. I was starting to get nervous. The only person I knew in this mansion was my partner, and I had no idea where he was. More to the point, he didn't know where *I* was.

I guess the guy thought all his animal talk was foreplay, because all of a sudden he grabbed my ass and planted his big sloppy mouth on mine. "This is what you came here for, isn't it?" he mumbled.

I struggled to get loose. As he tried to see how far down my throat he could put his tongue, I worked my way across the wall and over to an open window I had spotted. I knew that if I screamed, I would blow the operation, so I did the only thing I could think of to get someone's attention. I threw my big straw hat out the window. It must have been my lucky night, because my partner, who had gone outside to the pool to look for me, saw the hat come sailing out. Seconds later he burst into the room where I was still playing cat and mouse with the animal-lover.

He played the jealous husband to perfection, with a twist. "Hey, we're supposed to be doing this together. Why didn't you tell me you had already started." He distracted the guy long enough to let me pry myself loose. Then my partner became more abusive to me. "We came over here for *pleasure*. If you're going to pick up tricks yourself, baby, I'm gonna start charging the usual rate."

Now I was a hooker and my partner was my pimp.

"Buddy, if you're gonna mess with my lady here, I'm gonna have to charge you," Dave said to the guy.

Now we were talking that creep's language. "Hey, I don't need to pay you for any women. I've got a whole house full of them working for me down on Hollywood Boulevard." He proceeded to tell us exactly where his whorehouse was and how well he ran it. My partner winked at me. We'd gotten what we came for and a lot more.

We busted the group sex house a week later, and about a month after that I paid the animal-lover a visit at his place of business. This time I went with another partner and pretended to be looking for work. I had dumped my old pimp, and this guy was my new one, I explained. It occurred to me that we might all do some business together.

I went off with some of the hookers to see the house. They told me the house specialties and showed me the different rooms. There was one for animals (he wasn't kidding about that) and another where the whips and chains were kept. In one room there was a swing suspended from the ceiling; one of the hookers said that one of her customers liked to swing while she gave him a blow job. In another there was a huge hot tub, perfect for group sessions. Some of the johns really liked several women at once.

While I was being given the official house tour, my partner talked shop with the proprietor. The guy said he was thinking about raising prices and getting some more girls. He talked about the state of the economy and described his customers. In short, he gave my partner all the elements we needed to bust him. It took us about a week to make it official—I went back in there with a couple of female part-ners to get more evidence—but we ended up nailing the guy to the wall.

I've mentioned before that I've got my own private radar. Most of the time my ESP manifests itself in small ways. For instance, I'd be taking a police report from somebody, and I'd write down his date of birth before he told it to me. Once when I was working undercover in Vice I had an experi-ence—the kind that makes my daughter call me a witch— that was a full-scale save-my-ass type.

We were working a bar on Hollywood Boulevard, fol-lowing up on a complaint of prostitution and reports that drunks were being robbed. Things were going like clock-work, when all of a sudden I got a strong and distinct feeling about one of the guys sitting at the bar. I *knew* he had a gun on him. I also knew that if we brought down the bar the way we usually do, the guy would make our lives complicated and messy. (We don't usually search customers. We just clear people out once we have the ele-ments.)

I told my partner, Tony, I didn't feel right about this particular barfly and that I wanted to check him out. I walked over and operated him. Immediately I went straight into my dumb blonde hooker imitation. The guy instantly struck up a conversation with me—he had no idea I was a cop—and within a few minutes he had offered me money to have sex with him. When I got him outside where no one in the bar could see us, my partner and I arrested him. When Tony patted him down, he found the gun.

IN MY LAPD personnel file there are a lot of comments about the undercover work I did over the years. Browsing through it recently was like taking a wonderful trip down Memory Lane. "While working undercover, she successfully operated potential bookmakers, reducing the time normally required by male officers to make contact with and gain their confidence," says one entry from Sergeant Brian. "She arrested a significant number of tricks, assisting the unit in suppressing street prostitution," says another from Sergeant Parks. And finally: "Policewoman Hays proved to be a valuable and reliable asset to the Vice Unit. Her efforts were greatly appreciated."

Thanks, guys. It was a pleasure. And I miss you all.

9

SEX ON
THE FORCE

*Camaraderie among employees is healthy for the
employing organization and a necessary ingredi-
ent in a successful, productive, and fulfilling occu-
pation.*

—FROM THE 1989 LAPD FIELD MANUAL
(RULE 271)

Cops make life-and-death decisions together. We
save each other's lives. We share a tedium and a
tension that other people can't begin to know, with our long
watches, our stakeouts, and our mind-numbing paperwork.
Cops speak a special language that only other cops can
understand and form deep personal attachments that civilians can't begin to comprehend.

Women on the force often get to know the men they work
with better, and sometimes more intimately, than even their
wives or girlfriends do. They see how men function in an

emergency, how they make decisions, how they feel about women, how they handle people, and how they feel about themselves. Brought together in close quarters, sometimes twenty-four hours a day for days at a time, men and women cops sometimes become as close as two people can ever get.

And that's one *hell* of a turn-on.

Cop movies and television shows lie about a lot of things (most things, I think), but there's one recurring theme in fictional renderings of police work that's not a lie, and that's the incredible closeness that develops between cops. Police officers, men and women alike, have emotional ties tighter than any I've ever seen or experienced elsewhere. (It's hard to imagine doctors or lawyers or even teachers—who go through the wringer in their own way, I know—being as tight as cops. But maybe they would be if they spent a few nights sitting up in a car or had people shooting at them.) What does all of this extraordinary, unique closeness add up to? Just what you would imagine—sex, and lots of it. Police work can be and often is an incredibly sexy business.

Cops tell each other things that they would never dream of saying to a wife or a husband or even a shrink. Over the last twenty years I've heard just about everything, and more than once. I've listened to stories about drinking problems, marital difficulties, terminal illness, and problems with the kids. Guys have confessed that they're scared to death of being a cop and have revealed to me that they're gay. One of my partners wet his bed until he was fifteen. Another told me he had become impotent and asked me for advice. Another told me he couldn't carry bullets in his gun any longer because he'd been born again. I've reached out and made a few confessions myself along the way.

That's the way cops are with one another. When we like one another and trust one another, there's nothing we can't say. I've always felt that the relationship between male and female cops is particularly close.

As you might expect, many wives don't take too kindly to the fact that their husbands are off having heart-to-heart talks with lady cops at the office instead of bringing their confidences home. They don't understand it, and they definitely don't like it. That reaction on the part of a wife or girlfriend sometimes makes cops feel even more isolated, more alienated from the outside world, and thus more inclined to turn to another cop to fill their needs. It isn't just their wives who don't understand them, as the cliché goes. When you're a cop, you sometimes begin to think that *no one* understands you. That's one reason why so many police officers have affairs.

Female police officers always have a ready supply of men. After all, men still outnumber women nearly three to one in the LAPD; when I first went on the job, the male-female ratio was even more lopsided. There were plenty of times when I was literally the only woman in the station for months at a time.

One of my best friends on the force, Sandy, always says, "If you wait long enough, any man on the job is available." She's not interested in forming a permanent attachment— she's too caught up in her work to be able to maintain a marriage, as she learned when her first marriage didn't work out—and she really enjoys having flings and relationships with some of her partners.

When I first joined the force, there was sex everywhere. Just as everyone knew that Code 7 was lunch, Code X meant time out for a visit between the sheets. Of course, that was in 1967, and there was a lot more sex around everywhere. Wife-swapping was surprisingly prevalent in the early seventies; if my husband and I had been interested in that scene, our dance card would have been filled every night with cops and their wives. I love sex, but I've always taken it too seriously to get involved with swapping or any other casual sex scene. Anything other than one-on-one smacks of show biz to me. I can do a striptease for a roomful of strangers without blinking an eye, but I'm too shy to sleep with strangers.

Back when I worked the Van Nuys Jail, I met a woman who must have set a record for sex on the job. She didn't really look the part. The last thing that anyone looking at her would think of was *sexy*. Her figure wasn't great, and her hairdo was severe. She didn't believe in makeup, and I remember thinking that her hair and face were just about the same color. She used to move around the jail with slow, deliberate movements—like a boat pulling into harbor. She was hardly most people's idea of a sex goddess.

One night she came to work extremely distraught; she told me and the other policewomen in the jail that she had just found out her husband was gay. She had been married to him for two years, but she never had a clue that he wasn't straight—until she walked in on him and the electrician who lived across the street getting it on in her nice cozy queen-size canopy bed. It turned out that he'd been carrying on with men for the entire time the two of them had been married.

When we heard the story, we were properly sympathetic to her troubles and made all the right noises. We told her not to worry, that there were plenty of men out there. She was sure to do better next time. Little did we know that she was way ahead of us. As she proceeded to tell us, her husband wasn't the only one in that marriage who'd been having affairs with a lot of different men. By the time our shift was over, we had learned it all—names, dates, places, preferred positions—and there was a *lot* to learn. It wasn't easy to impress us, but our attention was definitely held by the tales of her sexual exploits. One of my favorites was about how she used to meet one of the guys over on the men's side of the jail under the desk in the cafeteria a few times a week. Lunch never seemed quite the same to me again after that.

After I left the jail, I didn't see her again, but I kept track of her over the years and followed her career with more than passing interest. She specialized in working with partners who were married. She herself married the first partner she worked with after her divorce from her first husband. Because department policy decrees that a husband and wife aren't allowed to work in the same division, she got herself another partner—also married—and began an affair with him. This became her pattern. Get married, change partners, screw the partner, get him to leave his wife, leave her husband—and then she'd change partners and the game would begin again. By the time she was pensioned off due to mental stress, she'd been married and divorced five times. Even for a cop, that's a lot. I'm on my third marriage, and that seems like enough. Anything beyond that makes marriage seem like a hobby.

On the job today, all police officers are created equal. Everybody wears the same uniform—men's trousers, remember—and everybody supposedly is treated the same. Rules and regulations govern the way each police officer is treated. What rules can't and don't have any dominion over, however, is the way people feel about each other. For example, in the hypothetical male-female partnership, each partner does an equal share, and their roles are interchangeable. Gender supposedly has nothing to do with how a partnership functions. Back in the *real* world, however, *real* people can't help but allow the baggage of their personal lives to burden their professional lives, and there's always a certain amount of role-playing between a male and female partner.

Still, there is a lot less macho posing in most police partnerships than there is in the average marriage. In marriages the husband tends to want to be the decision-maker and the protector, and he usually expects his wife to look to him as a leader, at least to some extent. Cops, even cops with Neanderthal values, know that applying those kinds of attitudes in a police partnership can get them killed in a great big hurry. Male cops may feel bigger and stronger than their female partners (usually they are), but they still have to accept the fact that they're a team.

Some guys have a problem accepting a woman on equal terms, and I've always felt that adding sex to a relationship makes that balance even harder to maintain. I prefer not to have physical relationships with the men I'm working with, because I'm sure I'll get too emotionally committed and that it would affect my judgment.

I enjoyed the deep rapport that I had with several of my partners over the years. A special kind of trust and friendship developed, nurtured by the mutual pressure of doing our job together. To me it represented the best nonsexual male-female bonding. It raised the work above the level of just doing a job.

Not all female police officers I know agree with me, especially the single ones. They will pursue and bed a coworker just as many of the women in a normal workplace do. Most of them would rather take poison than *marry* a cop, though. After a few years of getting to know these guys all too well, they have few if any illusions left about them as marriage partners. For one thing, they know that their husbands would probably screw around at work.

I'VE ALWAYS BEEN comfortable around gay people. There are a number of them on the force. As for me, I discovered back when I was starting out I don't like women making unwanted moves on me any more than I like men doing the same thing. I *am* more uncomfortable when women come on to me. Men who have had gay men come on to them tell me they feel the same way. They usually react in anger: a logical reason why the department doesn't go out of its way to recruit gay men.

When I was a rookie working the jail, there was a very intense gay officer in charge of my training. I was very put off when I first saw her. Her hair (which was never washed) hung in long, greasy strings, and her uniform looked like it belonged to a bag lady. She smelled like a fermented bottle of men's cologne. In her late forties, she looked almost exactly like a frog. There I was, straight out of the Police Academy, naive as hell. This woman took one look at my shiny face and hair and my neatly pressed uniform, and she was in love. It was like something right out of *Babes Behind Bars*.

I avoided her as much as I could, but one terrible night I was sitting on a high stool at a counter learning how to book someone into the jail. I was concentrating so hard on getting every detail right that I didn't notice the Frog Princess from Hell come up behind me. I had crossed my legs and swung them out from under the counter. She moved over next to me and pretended to be doing a jail count. I felt my whole body turn red as I realized she had spread her thighs and was rubbing herself on my leg.

I just kept on taking information from the prisoner—who couldn't see what was happening and must have wondered why my face was so red—and typing it on the form. Because I was new, I wasn't supposed to talk to anyone or otherwise allow myself to be distracted while doing the booking. Even under duress, I was determined to do my job by the book. She was my training officer, and I was still on probation, so

I felt trapped, embarrassed, horrified. She never even looked at me. She just kept rubbing, pretending that nothing out of the ordinary was happening.

Several days later, when I could finally talk about what had happened without stuttering, I made a complaint to my sergeant, a male. I stammered something like, "I do not want to work with her again. She rubbed herself all over my leg!" He refused to take the complaint—putting it in writing, he said, would complicate everyone's life. It wouldn't look good on my record, he went on, if I made a complaint during my first months in the jail. It would indicate to someone looking at my package that I was difficult to work with, not very flexible. This was years before we had any protection from discrimination. He told me he would put me on a different shift and then attempted some humor. "You know, once you've had a woman, some say you never want to go back to men." I didn't say a word, but I can sure tell you what I was thinking: "Fuck you."

On reflection, I've noticed that the department has a tradition of placing police officers with odd kinks in their personality in the jail, the one place where suspects and cops have to interact the most intensely and for the longest period of time. I suppose the thinking is to get them off the streets where they might cause the most harm.

When we had altercations in the jail, there were sergeants who would stand back and simply watch while the women fought. "Hot damn," they seemed to be thinking, "there's a fight going down on the female side." They seemed to be like a lot of men, turned on by any form of female physical-ity. On the other hand, a lot of them were threatened by male gayness.

Cop shows on TV are always featuring stories about homosexuality in the police force. Usually they're about men, but once in a while there will be a subplot about a lesbian. These stories are usually about somebody's "big secret"; when the secret is uncovered and people find out that a cop is gay, they blow up his locker and no one will work with him.

When I first came on the job, if a man was proven to be gay, he was fired, immediately. Today the pressure is a lot more subtle. Legally, gay men can now serve on the force, but they had sure as hell better stay in the closet. One of my partners kept his "big secret" for years, but eventually everyone found out he was gay. That's how he and I came to be partners. No one else wanted to work with him. The department is a lot more comfortable pairing off a male homosexual with a woman partner, gay or straight.

I don't know what the statistics are on the sexual predilections of LAPD cops—if there are any such stats, I'm sure the department isn't very eager to have anyone know about them—but I'd say that the incidence of male homosexuality is about what it supposedly is in the population as a whole, maybe one in ten at the most. On the other hand, I'd estimate that the percentage of gay women on the force is a *lot* higher than the national average.

T HE ONLY SUPERVISOR I ever had an affair with was Allan, who became my second husband. We met in the jail when

he was a new sergeant assigned there for his year's probation. We worked the jail together for six months before
Allan was transferred. Then, after we were married, we
weren't allowed to work together anymore. But we still
managed to partner together in a patrol car a few nights a
week. That's when I found out firsthand that it's not a good
idea to sleep with the guy you work with. He was always
trying to protect me; he even tried to use his rank to do it.
Our lives on and off the job became entwined and, to say the
least, got extremely complicated. It was life in the very fast
lane.

There were plenty of guys on the force, partners and
others, who tried to persuade me to change my mind about
my policy of not sleeping with my partners. I never blamed
them for trying; after all, when two people become as close
as I did to some of the guys on the force, it's perfectly
natural for at least one of them to think it would be a good
idea to have sex. I got very good at saying no.

To my way of thinking, having sex with a partner is a bad
idea, but I'm all in favor of a certain amount of flirtation on
the job. As far as I'm concerned, flirting is just another tool
for communicating, and an effective one at that. It makes
the wheels spin more easily and the world go 'round. I love
flirting with men, partners included. I enjoy making a man
feel that he's attractive. If I can make a man think he's
desirable—that I appreciate him as a man—without feeling
that he has to go to bed with me, I think I've done my good
deed for the day.

I'm not one of the boys, and I never have been. The truth
is, there is more than a little of my burlesque dancer mother

in me; I enjoy the attention, as long as the situation is controlled and I can call the shots. When I work with a roomful of men in a detectives' squad room, the sexuality is there, always, and I think it's a lot of fun. Usually it's just talk, with a lot of suggestive comments flying around the room, each of the men trying to outdo the others in terms of raunchiness. There's also a lot of laughing. The guys know just how far they can go, and they don't push it. And I know that anytime I want to, I can make it stop.

I worked with a Vice cop once who was one of the big talkers of all time. He was buffed out, single, and half the women were a little bit in love with him. The guys told me that he was so in love with himself he would parade in front of the locker-room mirror after a shower, posing. He loved himself to death.

When we first worked together, he made a few passes at me. I have to say he had style. He didn't even try to suggest our coupling would be anything more than a wonderful opportunity for me to be allowed to feel his very well developed and disciplined muscles—*all* his muscles. He entertained me by going into great detail about his endurance and ability. As he talked, his voice low and suggestive, he would move closer. He was a real master. I told him I would never want to break up the great love affair he was having. When he demanded who I thought his affair was with, I said, himself. We became good friends and great partners undercover. I learned to trust his street smarts completely. That kind of relationship is a lot better—and lasts a lot longer—than sex.

I'm not crazy about direct confrontation, although I'm not afraid of a good fight. My way of defending myself or making a problem go away is to be manipulative. When a guy put the moves on me, sometimes I'd go into my dumb blonde routine and try to joke him out of it. "C'mon," I would tell him, "if I sleep with you, I'll have to sleep with *everybody*."

If that didn't work, I'd just laugh and be a little more direct. "Knock it off" usually was all anyone needed to hear.

Some of my potential suitors were more stubborn than others, but nearly everyone was able to take no for an answer. Every so often I would come up against someone, nearly always someone who outranked me, who just didn't speak my language.

When I was still in Van Nuys Community Relations, just a few years after I joined the force, the captain over there took a special interest in me. He used to take me out for Code 7 (lunch) all the time, always in his car and usually to an out-of-the-way spot. Sometimes he'd drive me through the hills, and we'd come back noticeably late. When I describe the situation now, I realize that I sound like a real idiot for not being suspicious of his motives at the time, but I wasn't, not a bit. I was so naive and, even more to the point, so uninterested in him that I had no idea of what he was up to.

After a few weeks of those long lunches—which were innocently boring—some of my patrol pals filled me in on the captain's scheme. He was going all around the station saying things like: "The rumors that Gayleen and I are having an affair are not true" and "No matter what you hear, I am not fucking Gayleen." Of course, there *weren't* any rumors, but by the time he was through denying them all over the place, he had everybody thinking that he was getting into my pants. He knew, after a while, that he didn't have a chance in hell of sleeping with me, so he settled for letting people *think* he was. I was being used to promote his sexual image—to make him look like a stud.

I'd like to be able to say that I scotched the rumors and found some way to put him in his place, but it didn't happen that way. I did request a transfer, but only after I was sadly convinced that everyone in the office thought I *was* screwing him. I didn't stick around to win the battle but I did live to fight another day. Sometimes that just has to be enough.

There were many things about the police department that I really liked, but I always thought that one of its best features was that I couldn't get fired just because I wouldn't go to bed with somebody. I could always transfer or switch shifts. One of the reasons I was happy to be out on the patrol desk was that out there in front of God and everybody no one could pin me into a corner or take me on long lunches or put me in a vulnerable position, at least not very easily or for very long. There was no way some captain was going to take me for a ride again. Even when I was loaned out to other departments, I tried not to stay longer than a few months. A moving target is a lot harder to hit.

I did have a lieutenant once who made my life hell because I wouldn't go to bed with him. He put the screws to me every way he could, using the system every step of the way. He'd tell the sergeants to watch me especially carefully and to come out and talk to me about any criticism they could muster. If I didn't dot every "I" and cross every "T," I would be sure to hear about it and do the appropriate penance. During a routine inspection one day, he had a sergeant give me demerits because my buttons didn't line up with my belt buckle. Again, my only recourse was to transfer out of his clutches, and that's what I did.

Another guy, a sergeant, was so horrible that I got on a different shift to get away from him. We were on night watch together for a few months, and this clown spent that whole time telling me how good (and how big) he was in bed, how many policewomen he had fucked, and exactly how much each of them liked it. In case his sexual prowess didn't impress me sufficiently, he also told me how much money he made in his moonlighting job and what a great shot he was. All in all, he was a real prince.

I could probably have put up with his boasting and his bullshit, but then he started coming on to me. How could I resist someone as fantastic in the sack as he was? he wanted to know. When I declined his suggestions, very politely under the circumstances (I thought I deserved a medal for not losing my lunch all over his uniform), he started making my life miserable. When I'd go into his office to ask for a day off or some such thing, all I'd get were leers and comments like, "Sure, Gayleen, but what are you going to do for me? A day off is worth at least one blow job, don't you think?" The guy was an obnoxious jerk, but he wasn't stupid. He always made these comments in the watch commander's office when there was no one else around.

I never complained. I learned early on in the job that it

doesn't do any good to complain. I can't say I wasn't angry then or that I'm not angry now at having been treated badly by a few guys, but I've never enjoyed direct confrontations. It's just not my style. I learned how to solve my problems my own way, which was to pretend I didn't give a damn about anything; people can't get at you, I discovered, if you make jokes all the time, hug everybody, and act as if life is wonderful. Hell, sometimes I'm even able to convince myself.

Besides, with a little luck, every once in a while I get even.

About ten years ago I had a sergeant who thought he was God's gift to women. There wasn't anything appealing about him that I could detect, but he thought he was a superstud, and he thought I was hot. He was constantly making suggestive remarks to me, usually where everyone could hear them, and he would also tell stories around the station that were designed to make everyone think he'd been fucking me. (As I recall, he had a lot to say on the subject of whether I was a natural blonde.) Believe me, he had no such luck, and this time everybody knew it.

Even if no one believed his bullshit, having to listen to those sexual innuendos every day and having to see him leer at me all the time was getting old. One day during roll call I got my revenge, and it was sweet.

The sergeant used most of this roll call to give us training in a new piece of equipment. When he had finished his lecture, he looked around at the thirty-some people in the room.

"Does anyone have a question?" he asked.

"I have a question, Sergeant," I said sweetly.

"Yes, Gayleen?" he answered, with his usual leer. "You know I'd do *anything* for you." He just never stopped being an asshole.

In my sexiest voice I asked him: "Sergeant, do you know what a woman sounds like when she comes?"

The guys started snickering, no doubt knowing what was about to happen, but the sergeant was too caught up in his own macho act to suspect foul play.

He gave me his most sexy look before he spoke: "No, Gayleen, I don't," he answered.

"Sergeant, I didn't *think* you did," I said.

I think that's the first time anyone ever got a standing ovation at roll call.

10

COBRA

When a need develops for a single use plan affecting more than a single bureau or when it is necessary to develop a major project within a limited time, it may be appropriate to assemble a task force whose staff is provided on loan from various divisions or bureaus.

—FROM THE 1989 LAPD FIELD MANUAL
(RULE 625)

N early everyone agrees that police work made a lot more sense in the old days, when a cop was assigned to a beat and was responsible for anything and everything that went down in his territory. Unfortunately, that system just doesn't work anymore, at least not in Los Angeles. The reason isn't very complicated; it's just a variation on the old supply and demand theory. The call load is too big, and the manpower supply is too small.

For example, the Van Nuys Division is about 30 square miles—512 surface street miles, as I remember it—with a population of about 250,000 people. In Van Nuys Division when I left the force, there were six basic cars per shift (some two-man cars, others with just one man), to cover the entire area. There were special units as well, such as report units, cars for emergency calls, and so on. They might bring the total number of cars on duty at any one time all the way up to fifteen.

Fifteen cars for 250,000 people: even if an overwhelming percentage of the populace are law-abiding citizens, we're still talking about a busy night's work. And Van Nuys is not unusual in its ratio of cops to civilians; it's the same story all over the city. With those numbers, it's no wonder that the beat cop went the way of the dinosaur. It's no wonder either that the department is always trying to come up with new ways to make the most effective use of its personnel, especially when a really big case comes along.

That's why COBRA—Covert Operations to Battle Recidivist Activities—was created.

COBRA was established nearly ten years ago, as a separate unit that reports directly, and only, to the deputy chief's office. The COBRA unit has always been small; there have never been more than ten people in all, each of them handpicked by the deputy chief as one of the most outstanding officers in the whole city. For once, politics had nothing to do with who was chosen—a COBRA cop made the cut on the basis of his Rating Reports, his shooting ability, and his personality.

Notice I say *his* shooting ability and *his* personality; the COBRA unit has always been a nearly all-male club. It was set up with approximately nine men and only one woman, and that's the way it has remained. Back in early 1989 COBRA's one woman went up in rank and became a detective, and that's when they called and said I could put my name in to apply. The deal was that I would try it for a month. If it worked out for them and for me, I'd stick around permanently. I had no idea that I was about to embark on the most exhausting, stimulating, intense month of my entire career. I was a token and proud of it.

COBRA was the most glamorous of all police assignments. Cops didn't *look* especially glamorous when they worked COBRA; I don't think I've ever seen a scuzzier looking group in my life. But the work they did and the way they did it was as exciting and as glamorous as it comes. As far as I was concerned, COBRA made *Mission Impossible* and *The Dirty Dozen* look like one of the duller episodes of *Little House on the Prairie.*

The mandate of COBRA was simple and straightforward: to seek out and arrest hard-core, dangerous criminals. COBRA's cases ran the gamut of crime—narcotics, vice, burglary, homicide, just about anything—and they usually got their cases when another division didn't have the ability or manpower to get a job done. For instance, somebody over in Vice would spend a week trying to nail some asshole and finally run out of time or energy or both. "Let's give it to COBRA and see what they can do with it," he'd say to his sergeant, and that was usually what happened. Or someone from Homicide would get information on the street that something big was about to go down. If Homicide didn't have the task force to handle it, they'd turn to COBRA for help. Sooner or later COBRA got everybody's overflow of hard-core criminal cases.

There has always been a very impressive success rate attached to COBRA; they tended to get the bad guys, sooner or later. This success did not come cheap, however. Overtime is a way of life in COBRA—especially with its routine around-the-clock stakeouts—and overtime translates into big bucks. From the beginning, the city found it almost impossible to tolerate the huge COBRA budget, and more than once steps were taken to disband the group. In the end, though, the truth was so obvious that even bureaucrats could see it: you can't put the drug dealers and addicts in jail by working from nine in the morning until six at night. What's more, murderers, burglars, armed robbers, and rapists almost always work the night shift.

At the time I was loaned to COBRA, I'd been working the patrol desk for a few months, sitting around on my butt all day in my neat little policewoman's uniform, taking burglary-from-vehicle reports, answering the phones, filling out forms, and slowly being bored to death. I needed a change. I was more than ready to be shaken out of my normal patterns. COBRA gave me a lot more than I bargained for.

First of all, there was no such thing as a schedule for a cop assigned to COBRA. When I went to work each day, I had no idea what time I'd be coming home or what shift I'd be working from one day to the next. We had days off, yes, but only when a job was done. There was no such thing as a weekend. There were no uniforms either; everyone in

COBRA worked in plainclothes, and I do mean *plain*. Most of the assignments we took on called for undercover work, so we had to dress the part. There's no way I could pass for an executive secretary.

The two staples of my COBRA wardrobe were a pair of faded, ripped-up jeans that I picked up for a quarter at a garage sale and half a dozen wigs that I would change into and out of a few times a day. My favorite was a wiry brown wig that a Mexican hooker gave me as a going-away present when she left the Van Nuys Jail, but I also had an Afro wig and a curly blond one that I especially liked.

On most of the assignments I had on the force I used to work on one case at a time, or two at the most, but that's not how it was on COBRA. On any given day we'd have a load of as many as five cases, and on some shifts we'd do something on each one. (That's where the different outfits and wigs came in. There were days I changed my costume three or four times.) Sometimes we'd all roll on the same thing, a robbery suspect, for instance. Other times maybe four of us would cut off and stake out a motel room to catch a suspected rapist. I never knew from one day to the next what the night would bring. The sergeant in charge of COBRA (he'd been there since the beginning, and he's still going strong) knew where everybody was and what everybody was doing, and he kept us from getting our signals crossed—we trusted him with our lives.

One of the big fears any undercover cop has is that the right hand won't know what the left hand is doing. When that happens, one of those hands can end up dead. Not long before I worked COBRA, a friend of mine on the force had a close call that fell into this category. Jerry was working the Greyhound bus station, and he came up against a guy the papers were calling the Alphabet Bomber. The Bomber got his name because he'd been planting bombs around town, mostly in the airports, and threatening to blow various spots to smithereens. He always called to notify the cops of where the bombs were hidden, and so far no one had been hurt. Criminal Conspiracy was in charge of the case, and they had gotten a call saying that the Bomber was threatening to put a bomb in the bus station.

Communications between units being less than perfect, Jerry didn't know anything about the call or the bomb. He happened to be standing in the lobby of the bus station when he saw a skinny guy with long hair walking around and looking guilty. The guy had a plastic bag in his hand, and he walked over to a trash can and tossed it in. He kept looking around all the time, as if he was making sure he wasn't being followed. Three possibilities leaped into Jerry's mind: one, the guy had ripped somebody off and was getting rid of the garbage; two, he was dropping narcotics; or three, he was getting rid of a gun or something he'd just stolen. Any one of the three was enough to persuade Jerry to move in and check him out.

He walked over to the suspicious character, identified himself as a police officer, and told him not to move. That's when the guy pulled the rug out from under him.

"You'd better make this look good. I'm with Criminal Conspiracy. I've got a forty-five here in my waistband, and there's another one in my leg holster." He told Jerry his name, rank—sergeant—and serial number.

Jerry went through the motions of searching the sergeant, handcuffed him, retrieved the bag, and walked him out of the station, where he learned that the plastic bag was full of money and the sergeant's assignment was to leave it for the Alphabet Bomber. The Bomber had been making his ransom phone calls from a hotel just down the street. The only problem was, no one had told Jerry anything about it.

One of the reasons COBRA is so successful is that they have a great system, which has been carefully worked out and refined over the years. (There's chaos, but it's well-organized chaos.) Every case is different, but the basic elements of how any operation is handled are similar. When I was there and we were staking out someone, there would always be at least four people involved in a case. A few blocks away from the scene there would be the *radio guy*, the person whose job it was to keep track of everyone's activities and maintain contact with the outside world. Then there was the *looker*, the one who would get in close to the action and signal the others. If there was likely to be any danger in the operation, there was also a *shooter*, who would cover the looker at all times and stay close to the action. The others are *backups*. Everybody has a job to do, and if everything goes the way it's supposed to—which it usually does—there won't be any surprises.

One of the most important things I learned on COBRA was that most hard-core criminals don't usually confine themselves to one kind of crime. For example, we could start out investigating a robbery and discover along the way that the guy we arrested was also a drug dealer. One night I was staking out a parking lot looking for a suspect in a narcotics case, and I walked by what appeared to be an empty van. Just as I came up alongside the van, I heard a squeaking sound. I stopped and listened long enough to establish that what I was hearing was an animal in distress. I knocked on the door of the trailer, but no one answered.

When I ran the number on the license plates, I discovered that the van had been stolen, along with the owner's two dogs. My partner and I got into the van and found the poor dogs, who had obviously been crying out of hunger and thirst. We also found a woman's underpants with blood still on them. After the lab was finished matching the blood type to a recent rape victim, we ended up arresting the guy for rape as well as theft.

Another time we were staking out a grocery store, and one of the COBRA guys' snitches, someone he'd arrested a few years earlier for dealing drugs, spotted him and told us about some gang activity that had been going on for a couple of weeks. One gang member was stealing stereos from all the other gang members in the neighborhood. We checked it out and learned that the stereo thief was also burglarizing houses *and* selling heroin to kids.

Still another time we were watching robbery suspects in a grocery store, three Mexican guys who had hit several places in the area. One of my partners was on the roof, and there were two more in the parking lot. I was the point man that night, so I walked into the store to see what was going on. I pretended to be a little drunk and bought a bottle of beer. As I opened the bottle and took a drink, I saw the suspects. They weren't robbing anyone; they were holding a little girl and talking to her in a very aggressive manner. She looked scared. I moved closer and listened. My Spanish is okay but not great, so I wasn't positive what they were saying, but I thought I heard them offering to pay her for sex.

I left the store and signaled to my partner on the roof, who spoke perfect Spanish. As he entered the store to see if my suspicions were correct, I went out back. Only a few minutes later, the three men and the girl walked out the back door and headed for a car that was parked thirty feet away. They were practically dragging the girl with them. By the time they got there, our whole team surrounded them. My partner had heard their plans quite clearly: they were going to give the girl (who, we later learned, was thirteen) five dollars to give each of them a head job. We made the arrest.

Once in a while this "small world" aspect of crime would complicate my life, like the time I was working stolen-car suspects and I walked in on some robbery suspects I'd busted a week before. It was a case of wrong time, wrong wig—I was wearing the same undercover clothes and wig I'd worn to bust them earlier.

"That bitch is the heat!" one of them said when he saw me.

"No problem," I said, smiling as brightly as I could while fingering my .38 and hoping my partner would come back as soon as possible. "Even cops get a day off."

Luckily they laughed and let me get the hell out of there.

Another time I had to stake out the high school in my own neighborhood, less than three blocks from where I live. One afternoon I was sitting in my car in full COBRA regalia—cutoffs, a fringed T-shirt with holes in it, and my cowboy hat—and one of my neighbors walked by. I was wearing one of my many wigs, but she recognized me anyway. When she started to approach me, I said something rude to get rid of her. "Hey, baby, get lost" is what I think I came up with. She stormed away in a huff, and my cover was safe.

I have always had a tendency to lose weight if I'm under any kind of pressure. When I worked COBRA, the pounds just fell off me. Part of the reason was tension, but the other part is that I was constantly starving to death; I could never find anything halfway decent to eat when we were on stakeouts. Most of the guys would eat just about anything. Their idea of the four food groups was salt, cola, sugar, and saturated fat. Junk food has never agreed with me, so I used to try to take along food with some actual nutrients whenever I went on a stakeout. (I think it's safe to say I was the only COBRA cop who regularly carried a baked potato in her purse.) To make matters even tougher, when I did finally find something to eat, more often than not it was time to roll.

I'll never forget the night I had finally scored the perfect piece of chicken. It wasn't fried or breaded or covered in grease; it was just juicy and flavorful, exactly the way I like it. We were staking out a second-story rapist at the time, and our suspect was a guy who worked security on the three to eleven shift. After work he would drive over to an area where a lot of nurses lived, break into their apartments, and be waiting for them when they got home, after their night shifts. We had a good description and a partial license plate, and we were pretty sure we wouldn't have to wait too long for the guy to show. I was going to act as decoy.

Just as I was about to take the first bite of my perfect chicken, the looker gave the signal we had all been waiting for. The suspect's car had been spotted, and he was getting ready to pull into a parking place. It was time for me to walk down the street toward him to view the upcoming crime.

I reached him just as he was getting out of his car, and what I saw was enough to make the arrest. He was wearing a mask and gloves, and in his right hand was carrying a small piece of rope. I could see a knife in his belt.

We could have let him go on and break into the apartment. Our case would have been even stronger if we watched him commit a few more crimes, but not only is it illegal, it's against our consciences to let someone become a victim just to make a case stick in court. We knew from experience that if we let him out of our sight, we wouldn't be able to control the situation. Since the evidence we already had was enough to prove intent, and since we knew that the victims would be able to pick him out of a lineup, we decided to call it a night. I gave the signal, and we made the arrest.

When I got back to the car, someone had eaten my chicken.

Much of the work that COBRA does is undercover, and that means surveillance, surveillance, and more surveillance. As action-packed and exciting as COBRA was, it also involved more sitting around and waiting for something to happen than I have ever experienced. There were days we followed suspects all over town as they went about their relatively normal lives. After all, even criminals have to buy groceries, go to the bank, and pick up their laundry. If they're hungry, they eat, and once in a while they even take in a movie. And if they did any of those things while they were under surveillance, we got to watch them do it. We spent half our lives sitting in cars.

One of the best ways to pass the time under those circumstances was to keep talking. On a long shift we would cover just about every topic you can imagine, but being cops, we always came back to our favorite subject: the art and science of catching assholes. COBRA guys loved to talk shop. I still remember one of the smartest comments I heard during that time. It was made in the middle of the night during a long date-rape stakeout.

"Criminals are like animals. They like to use the same game trail," one of my partners, George, told me. "If a crook is good at something, he'll do it over and over again until he gets scared or gets caught. Take a bank robber, for instance. If all he ever uses is the demand note saying that he's got a bomb, he's gonna continue to use that same pattern until he gets caught—or comes so close that it scares him. Hell, he might even use the same demand note. Some of these guys are incredibly consistent in what they do, and that's often how you nail 'em. It gets so you can say, 'He's gonna hit this block on Tuesday between these two hours,' and sure enough, he hits it, because he'd been hitting a house in that area every Tuesday for the last two months. The criminal who *won't* get caught is one who doesn't develop a pattern, the guy who tries something once or twice and then moves on to something else."

Sure enough, that thinking paid off on the date-rape case. The guy came back, just as George predicted.

There is an undeniable air of the renegade about a lot of the COBRA guys, and as you can imagine, it got on the nerves of a lot of the pencil pushers on the force. Still, in spite of their bold and sometimes unorthodox ways, COBRA played it strictly by the book. I found that out firsthand one night when we had to let a bad guy get away. We'd been staking out a convenience store because we had a tip there was going to be a 211 (robbery with a gun) there that night.

Sure enough, the suspect showed up on schedule, and my partner and I walked into the back of the store to check him out while a couple of other COBRA guys waited outside. When it was time to move in, when we had *incontrovertible evidence that a robbery was being committed,* I was supposed to give them a signal. (If we had less than incontrovertible evidence, it wouldn't stand up in court. That was quite a system. I used to think that we had to wait until someone was actually murdered before we could intervene.)

We blew it. The robber's back was to my partner, so he couldn't see whether the suspect had his gun out or not. My partner thought the guy was threatening the cashier, so he yelled at him. It turned out no threat had been made. The suspect was prevented from crossing that fine line. We knew that he had been about to commit a robbery, but we couldn't be a hundred percent sure we could make it stick. We didn't have quite enough to prove intent. We were able to book him for carrying a concealed, unregistered weapon for which he didn't have a permit (big surprise), but armed robbery would have been a lot better. It never occurred to anyone on the detail that night to try to play fast and loose with the Field Manual.

I love chaos. My house and my car are always a complete mess, and that's exactly how I like it. My favorite "Peanuts" character has always been and will always be Pigpen. But certain kinds of chaos are harder for me to take than others. The kind of chaos that COBRA thrived on—the juggling of cases and the constant excitement—nearly wiped me out.

I was a complete wreck when I worked COBRA. I didn't notice it right away because I was having too good a time; I couldn't *wait* to get to work every day. But after a while I couldn't help but see that the excitement of the job was taking its toll on me. Moving from case to case kept me wired to the max, and unlike the other guys, I didn't find it easy to relax. When I got home, I was too stoked to sleep for more than a few hours, so my eyes were red all the time. I was getting dangerously thin. And my family life wasn't exactly idyllic; who wants a wife and mother who's continually connected to not one but two radios (one in my car and one on my person) and who's on call twenty-four hours a day?

The hectic, frenzied pace could cause major screwups.

One time we were in the middle of a drug bust; we were chasing the suspect out the back door of his hideout. I was the first one out the door after him, and I didn't notice that a piece of the porch was sticking up just beyond the threshold. I caught my foot and went sprawling, landing flat on my face.

I was humiliated, but at least I had the presence of mind to get the hell out of the way before my fellow officers walked all over me. I threw myself to the side just seconds before the giant boot of my partner would have been planted squarely on my head.

I caught up with my fellow COBRAs just as they were putting the cuffs on the dealer.

"Nice block, Hays," was all anyone said about it.

I'D ALWAYS HEARD about the concept of penis envy, but it wasn't until I worked COBRA that I really began to accept it. I don't think that my take on the idea is the same as Freud's, however. My theory is more practical than psychological; when you're on a stakeout, a penis makes it a hell of a lot easier to take a leak, and it would have been pretty nice to have one. If I had a nickel for every guy who went out behind a tree and relieved himself while I sat in the car in complete agony, I'd be in fat city.

One night we were on a stolen-car stakeout that had been dragging on for days, and I really had to go. I couldn't bring myself to visit one of the nearby trees; I've never been very comfortable peeing in the great outdoors. I told my partner that I was going to make a run for it. There was a gas station a half mile down the road; I'd take my car—he and I were traveling in separate cars that night—and be back before he knew it. After all, we had been staking out this guy for days. Leaving for ten minutes couldn't hurt anything. I took off. You can probably guess what happened.

I drove as fast as I could down the dark side road and walked into the filthiest ladies' room I have ever seen. All of a sudden the great outdoors seemed pretty appealing, but I decided to settle for what I had. I had just dropped my jeans and was getting into position when a voice came over my radio.

"We're moving," said the guy in charge of the case.

Personally, I wasn't really in much of a position to move, but I did so, and fast. For almost a week I had been waiting for the payoff on that stakeout, and I was damned if I was going to be in that hellhole when it finally went down. I was tired, but I was still fired up, even at five o'clock in the morning.

I must have set a land speed record for urinating. Within seconds I had yanked up my jeans and was in my car, trying to catch up with the convoy of undercover cars, which was now pursuing the suspect to another part of the Valley. I made it in plenty of time, and we nailed the guy just the way we'd planned. As a special reward, the guys told me that I could be the one to put the handcuffs on the suspect.

I was honored. But soon my pleasure turned into confusion. The problem was, I didn't seem to *have* my handcuffs. All of a sudden I remembered hearing a small clinking sound when I pulled on my jeans in that gas station and dashed out in such a hurry. Unless I was badly mistaken, those handcuffs were on the wet, horrible floor of the most disgusting gas station bathroom in California history. I didn't tell anyone about my suspicions, though. These were the same guys, remember, who had seen me take a header out the door during the drug bust. I didn't feel like giving them any more to ride me about. I quickly borrowed my partner's handcuffs and did the honors.

A few minutes after that I realized that my handcuffs weren't the only important pieces of official police equipment I no longer had with me. I didn't have my badge either. Missing handcuffs are relatively easy to explain and replace, but if there's one thing the department doesn't take kindly to, it's a missing badge. And mine was the only one of its kind, an endangered species.

I hopped into my car and drove back the way I'd come, even faster this time, across the Valley. It was nearly eight in the morning by then, and the traffic was already bumper to bumper. Everybody was awake now, and I had a terrible feeling that I wasn't going to get there in time. When I finally reached the grungy gas station, I ran inside the ladies' room and rummaged around on the floor. There they were, the tools of my trade, my handcuffs and my badge, sitting in what I knew was a pool of urine. I picked them up gingerly and walked back to my car. All in all, it had been quite a night.

COBRA

· · · · ·

I T WAS OBVIOUS that COBRA was not going to be my life's work, but I loved it. I don't think I've ever felt happier about being a cop. Unfortunately, the COBRA life-style didn't allow me enough time to devote to my family. The choice between the two was a difficult one—although I've never regretted mine.

The day I left COBRA was one of the saddest of my career. I would have loved to stay there forever, standing out on the edge of the precipice, not knowing what the next moment, let alone the next day, was going to bring. It would have been great to work night watch and morning watch for the next ten years and swap stories with the toughest, nicest guys I ever worked with. And it would have been great to go home every day feeling as if what I had done made a real difference.

Some people do work COBRA for years at a time, and I think I know their secret. The guys who make it in COBRA are the ones who pace themselves. They can work one case, then take a break, work out, play raquetball, have a beer, before going on to the next case. They don't fly from place to place and throw themselves headlong into every assignment. They don't treat every case as if it's a matter of life and death, even when it is. And they probably don't lose their handcuffs and do pratfalls when they get tired.

I envied the COBRA cops and admired them, but I knew I could never be like them. So I went, for a time at least, back into uniform. My husband and daughter were glad to have me back in the real world.

TOOLS OF
THE TRADE

In a complex urban society officers are daily confronted with situations where control must be exercised to effect arrests and to protect the public safety. Control may be achieved through advice, warnings, and persuasion, or by the use of physical force.

—FROM THE 1989 LAPD FIELD MANUAL (RULE 240.10)

The first time I ever fired a gun—on my very first day in the Police Academy—I fell in love with the way it made me feel. That night I called my grandmother and told her the big news.

"Grandma, it's *amazing*," I said. "They gave me this gun to shoot, and I wasn't at all nervous. It felt perfectly natural in my hand. Can you believe it?"

Grandma wasn't a bit surprised. "It runs in the family," she explained. "Every woman in the family knows how to shoot. Your great-grandma was the best shot in Tillamook County."

When it comes to the skills, talents, and predilections of the women in my family, I have learned to expect the unexpected. However, I had no idea until that conversation that I come from a long line of females who are handy with a gun. It was quite true what I told my grandmother that day: I wasn't the least bit afraid of guns. The first time I held a gun in my hand, I felt as if it belonged there. What's more, I turned out to be a very good shot.

At the Police Academy we shot an hour a day, every day, and that was far and away my favorite part of the entire training. I even liked the part where we cleaned our guns and learned how to take them apart and put them back together again. I enjoyed the ritual of loading and unloading and counting the bullets. But what I really liked was the shooting.

At first I shot left-handed—I do most things left-handed—but my spent shells used to fly out and hit my neighbor, Shilah, on the side of her head. A week into my training I switched to shooting with my right hand and have stayed with it ever since. The training was rigorous, and the grading was strict. Anyone who was unable to reach a certain score, which was relatively high, wasn't allowed to graduate. All the women in my small class made it, but I've since heard of Academy students, both male and female, whose shooting ability wasn't up to par and who didn't graduate because of it.

Speaking of male and female shooters, I have always thought that women are marginally better shots than men. I don't know why, of course. However, my guess is that men, because they're more inclined than women to believe that brute strength will win the day, tend to jerk back the trigger, while women usually squeeze it more gently. Squeezing the trigger, as if you're squeezing a lemon, definitely results in greater accuracy. To fine-tune your aim even more you can do what I did—put a little chalk dead center on the sight of the gun to make it that much easier to line up with the target. We trained in two kinds of shooting, target and combat. Target shooting is exactly what it sounds like; you stand in one place and shoot at a stationary target. In combat shooting, the target moves, approximating as closely as possible the conditions of combat itself, except, of course, that the targets don't shoot back or call you a motherfucker. Police Academy students have to be good at both kinds. We also had to learn how to use a shotgun, my favorite.

The first gun I ever shot is the one I have now, a .38 Smith & Wesson, serial number K851141. I've had it for more than twenty years, and I've never once been tempted to make a switch. Along the way most police officers have changed to automatic weapons, but I never liked automatics, and not just because I'm not wild about flying with the flock. Automatics are a lot heavier and bulkier, and they don't have that little telltale "bump" that my .38 has. When I put my finger on the trigger of my .38 and pull back, there's a little bump I can feel. If I'm pressed for time, I can pull back fast as far as the bump without actually firing the gun, and from there I squeeze. To me that bump is the point of no return.

For many years people tried to get me to switch to an

automatic, but I always refused to give in. I like the feel of the .38. After a while I couldn't have switched guns even if I'd wanted to, because by then I was superstitious. How could I be expected to give up a gun that had served me so well for so many years? I would be asking for trouble.

Dirty Harry always used a .44 Magnum because, as I remember from the movies, he didn't want to take a chance on missing anything when he shot. That's how I feel about the shotgun. The spray of bullets that a shotgun puts out hardly makes it a sophisticated weapon, but there's something more than a little comforting about knowing that when you use a weapon, you are simply *not* going to miss your target. In the heat of battle, when a cop's adrenaline is pumping and there's chaos all around, the relatively low margin of error of the shotgun can mean the difference between life and death. And even when you don't use it to shoot *at* someone, the booming sound of a shotgun can be very handy for scaring the hell out of people. If nothing else, it gets their attention in a hurry. However, cops never shoot to warn.

Some people think that a police officer's weapons training ends with graduation from the Police Academy, but that couldn't be further from the truth. The pressure on a cop to maintain his or her shooting skills never lets up. In fact, every cop on active duty is tested once a month, when he has to revisit the Police Academy and "qualify." Toward the end of any given month, "I have to go qualify" is the phrase on nearly everyone's lips. Like every other group of people in the world, cops put their obligations off until the last minute, so on the last day of the month the line that forms for people who need to qualify is something to behold. I know. I've stood in it many times.

One month we had to qualify for target shooting; the next month our combat skills were tested. (I always preferred combat shooting, because it was outdoors and a little more challenging.) We used to have to qualify every month, but then the department, trying to save a few bucks, changed it to every month. The regulations regarding qualifying have always been very strict. Everyone has to go every month— no exceptions—and the scores required are quite demanding. If at first someone didn't succeed, he could try again, but only after going to the end of the line. Anyone failing to show up had to take a day off without pay. Anyone showing up but failing to qualify was subjected to a full-fledged investigation. The police force takes shooting seriously.

Shooting has always been easy for me. In the Academy I always shot the highest scores, and qualifying was never a problem either. I looked forward to going to the Academy to shoot; to me it was Old Home Week. Not everyone has my attitude, though. Some of my fellow officers really dreaded having to qualify, especially the lousy shots. One cop I know, Danny, was such a terrible shot that he had to get drunk before he could qualify. He was a crack shot when he'd had three or four belts. (Fortunately, he had a desk job. The only time he ever had to use his gun was when he qualified.) It wasn't unusual for some guys to go through the line two or even three times before getting a high enough score. Once in a while someone had to be talked through the test by a training officer.

If going to the Academy to qualify was Old Home Week to me, Training Day was a high school reunion. Once a year all the cops in a given division would be called together for Training Day, a full day of learning and interaction. (If we were priests, I suppose it would be called a retreat.) Some of it was social—at the end of the day there was always a big steak fry—but there was also a full agenda, dictated by the captain: refresher courses in routine police work; instruction in new techniques, new equipment, and new laws; and training exercises. Some guys hated Training Day, but I always looked forward to it. Whether it was fashion shows, stakeouts, or Training Day, I've always enjoyed the company of other cops.

Even when shooting or handling a gun doesn't come naturally to a cop, as it did to me, it doesn't take very long for a gun to become first a habit and then an integral part of a cop's life. After a short time I didn't even think of it as a weapon, any more than a carpenter considers his saw or his chisel a weapon. For a cop a gun is a tool. I don't think I ever felt so aware of this fact as when I reached for mine and found that it wasn't there.

Right after I left the Van Nuys Jail, I worked in Community Relations, giving safety lectures in the community and visiting schools. My partner and I were on our way to make a speech one day, and as we were leaving the school auditorium where we held forth on the glories of self-protection, we got a call on the radio about a 211 (armed robbery) going down in the neighborhood. A young guy was in the middle of robbing a market about a block away. We took off for the market and rolled up in the back. Naturally, we didn't use our sirens.

My partner and I were in our meet-the-public uniforms, not exactly dressed to arrest bad guys. I had on my skirt, dress jacket, and high heels, and I was carrying my policewoman's purse. We jumped out of the car and moved to get into position—on the side of the car behind the door, for protection—but before we were quite ready, the suspect came running out. He already had a head of steam up. He was *very* surprised to see us.

"You're under arrest," my partner yelled to him. To back him up I reached into my purse for my gun.

The problem was, the gun wasn't there. I didn't *have* a gun.

The suspect did. He wasn't pointing it at me yet—he was still too stunned to see us there—and in that split second he had to decide whether to go for it or fold his cards. My partner didn't have a clear shot; too many people were coming out of the market. *I* had the shot—but nothing to shoot with.

"Shit!" I shouted. That response was not dictated by the Field Manual, but it clearly stated my innermost feelings.

This was another example of the importance of a cop's ESP. My partner somehow sensed that I was less than fully armed. Without missing a beat and before the suspect knew that I was in trouble, my partner pulled *his* gun and saved my ass.

Fictional cops almost always get killed in big shootouts or

dramatic busts, but in the world that's not made for TV, cops get killed by making mistakes just like the one I made that day. There was a simple explanation for why I didn't have my gun. When I gave self-protection speeches, I used to turn my purse upside down when I showed the women in the audience how to carry their purses. When I first started doing it, my gun would fall out and scare some people. So I took to putting the gun in a different purse and leaving it in the backseat during the lectures. That's where my gun was when the suspect came barreling out of that door.

Of course, all the logical explanations in the world couldn't have saved me that day if my partner hadn't been alert. If the robbery suspect had had the presence of mind to shoot me, I'd be dead meat. Even the best shot in the world can't do anything without a gun.

I was incredibly grateful to my partner for saving me. It took me quite some time to stop thanking him every day and trying to find ways to repay him. I was relatively new on the force at the time, so I didn't know what all cops learn sooner or later, that saving your partner's ass is all part of the job. No thank-you notes are necessary.

A year or so later I had my own chance to come to the aid of a partner in a significant way. I was just a temporary partner; his regular one was out sick for a few days. The two of us had been to the Academy together to qualify, and on the way back to the division we got a call to check out a bomb threat in a bank. According to our information, it was probably just a hoax. Otherwise the bomb squad would have handled the call.

As we walked through the bank I spotted a small brown

paper bag that didn't seem to belong to anyone. I asked a few people about it; no one seemed to know whose it was or what was in it. This wasn't any big-deal bank with political connections or anything. It was just a little savings and loan. But I still didn't like the look of that bag. I wanted to call the bomb squad and have them check it out.

My partner was being very blasé about the whole thing. He had been called on a lot of these bomb threats—many more than I had—and he didn't take it very seriously. "It's probably just some candy bars or something," he said.

He didn't seem to take *me* very seriously either. When I said again that we should call the bomb squad, he suggested that we just look in the bag, throw it away, get out of there, and go to Code 7. We ended up doing something that cops are never supposed to do. We had an argument in front of civilians.

I started it. "If you go near that bag, I'm going to clear everybody out of this bank. You're going to feel like a real asshole if it goes off," I told him.

"You're the one who's being an asshole," he replied. "I've handled calls here before. This is just some chicken-shit thing. There's no bomb in that bag. Trust me."

I was beyond caring about trust. I didn't want him to touch the damn bag.

I won the argument. We sent for the bomb squad. They evacuated the bank and found a homemade bomb in the bag. My partner was quiet. That was enough thanks for me.

The worst question you can ask a cop is the one people ask most often.

"*Have you ever shot anyone?*" There isn't a police officer alive who likes to hear that.

It's natural for civilians to be curious, but if they knew how painful the subject is for most cops, they'd keep their curiosity to themselves. At least I hope they would.

Cops don't even ask each other about shootings, because most of us know what it means to shoot somebody. They might say something like, "Was it a good shooting?" Just after an incident has taken place, but that's the closest they come to prying. A cop might volunteer the information in conversation sometimes, with a cathartic, "I shot the asshole, and it was a good shooting," but I've never seen a cop who was happy about shooting somebody. And I've never known anyone who, having shot someone, could just forget about it, either. I don't think I'd want to know anyone who could.

Twenty years ago the LAPD was completely different from the way it is today. The department's approach to dealing with criminals was different, the kind of crime we had was different, and—perhaps most significant of all—the tools of the trade were different. There were pistols and shotguns, of course, but we didn't have chemical Mace, we didn't have tasers (the official name for what most people call stun guns), and we didn't have a lot of the other auxiliary devices used to control prisoners. We were given more freedom to search and seize, more freedom to decide when a crime had been committed and when physical force was needed. But that's not the way it is anymore.

Many people think that the reason for the changes is that cops simply aren't as big and strong as they used to be. Mace and tasers and the like are meant to take the place of muscle. Think about it. In the old days a cop had to be five feet, ten inches tall. That was eventually lowered to five eight, then to five six, and finally all the way down to five feet tall. There are police officers on the force today who are five feet tall and weigh less than a hundred pounds. It's no wonder that the LAPD doesn't encourage them to mix it up. Mace, nightsticks, tasers, and other kinds of equipment are the equalizers.

One of the standard weapons in our hand-to-hand combat arsenal in the old days was what we referred to as the bar-arm-control—the choke hold. The choke hold worked like a charm; 99 percent of the time, an obstreperous prisoner quit fighting as soon as a cop applied the choke hold, for at least as long as it took to put some handcuffs on him. But some years ago, after a few people were badly hurt and a couple of them died as a result of the choke hold, the hold was outlawed by the LAPD.

Personally, I think outlawing the hold was a big mistake. It's a very effective hold for control purposes, even if a cop isn't particularly strong, and under normal circumstances it's harmless. It just puts people out of commission for a few seconds. I won't try to dispute the fact that some people died as a result of the choke hold, but what people don't seem to understand is that those who died were extremely violent suspects completely strung out on PCP. PCP is a drug that masks pain, gives users superhuman strength, and causes the adrenaline to increase. The people who got hurt didn't have the sense to stop fighting, and they ended up having the small bones in their voice boxes broken. That breakage causes swelling, which in turn closes off the breathing passage.

Taking the place of the choke hold these days is the baton, or nightstick. There's nothing very subtle about the stick. You just haul back and hit people with it. During training we were taught a very stylized, almost balletic way of using the stick—lunge and withdraw—but the truth is, when the action starts, there's barely enough time—mere seconds—to get the stick out, let alone to lunge and withdraw. Whenever I looked at my stick, which I always kept in the back of my car, I'd remember those times after roll call when we'd line up and whack a punching bag as hard as we could with our sticks. Somehow it didn't seem like real police work to me.

I'm trained in the use of the taser, too, but I've never been a big fan. For one thing, it's not very reliable. If a suspect is psychotic or stoned on drugs or even extremely sweaty (in my experience, most criminals are all three), it just doesn't work. For another thing, it's more than a little scary. Just ask any cop who's been zapped himself.

One day several years ago I was on the way to an under-cover site with three other police officers, all sergeants. Two were in the front seat, and I was in the back with the other.

We had just had dinner, and my neighbor, who was fooling around with his taser gun, accidentally hit the sergeant in the front seat, the one who was driving, right in the back of the neck. Fortunately he was driving very slowly at the time, because it knocked him out cold. He told us later that he had never experienced anything like it in his life. When that electrical current went through his body, he thought he'd had a massive heart attack. He was sure he was a goner. I haven't had much of a taste for the taser ever since.

I'm not much fonder of Mace. I've used it and seen it used, and the only effect that I've consistently observed is that it made *me* temporarily blind, no matter how or where it was used. Using it outdoors is especially messy; it seemed to me that any time anyone used the stuff, it found its way back into my eyes. Mace and I go way back together. My first experience with it came when I was working the jail and a female prisoner was brought in on a warrant. I was training another policewoman in the finer points of conducting a search, and the policewoman—not the brightest student I've ever had—picked up a can of Mace, said, "What's this?" and sprayed it right in my face.

THERE ARE MANY things in police work that change. There are new methods, new rules, new lieutenants, even a new chief every once in a while. But there's one thing that never changes: roll call. Every shift starts with roll call, a forty-five-minute psychodrama in which almost anything can happen and often does. It's not *so* different from what you used to see at the beginning of *Hill Street Blues*.

Roll call is where we would hear what went down while we were off duty and be brought up to date on the latest crime waves in the division. It's where we would get trained in the latest equipment and find out about changes in the law. It's where we would listen to speeches and see videos—about search and seizure, for instance, or a shooting in another city—so that we could learn from other people's failures and successes. Some days we'd have show and tell; for example, one of the specialists in gang activities would give us the latest scoop on the gangs and show us some of their state-of-the-art weapons.

Roll call was a peculiar combination of the formal and the informal. There were rules galore about behavior in roll call. First, we were not allowed to be late, ever, not even a minute. No excuses were accepted, and anyone who broke that rule got into serious trouble. Second, we had to be in clean, well-pressed uniforms. Most of the time people abided by this rule, but not always; over the years I saw (and wore) just about everything. Once, when I was working undercover for a stretch, I woke up, went to the closet to get my uniform, and remembered that I'd left it back in my locker. I knew I couldn't be late, so I showed up on time, but in my bathrobe. Third, we weren't supposed to do anything that might be distracting while roll call was going on, such as eat, read the paper, tell dirty jokes, or do our nails. The enforcement of that rule was completely dependent on the sergeant in charge. Some of them were reasonable; others were hard asses from the word go.

Hard ass or not, most sergeants held inspection every Friday after roll call. It was a lot like being in the Marines, or at least the way movies always portray what being in the Marines is like. We would all stand in a line, and the officer in charge would walk slowly along and give us the once-over, first in front and then behind us. (When being inspected, we were forbidden to look directly at the person giving the inspection. We were told to look at the center of his chest.) In my full policewoman's uniform I wore a skirt, regulation shoes, a shirt with hash marks, a tie, and a hat. On my belt, I carried my gun and holster, handcuffs, tear gas, extra bullets, notepad, and keys to the callbox. I also had a name tag, business cards, an ID card, a driver's license, and, of course, my badge. We almost never show our badges on the job. If we're out of uniform and need to show our identity, we flash our ID.

Usually the inspection would be confined to uniforms, guns, and a routine check of driver's licenses and other papers, but once in a while, when the sergeant was a pain in the ass or, more often, when somebody had been leaving food in his locker overnight, we had to go through locker inspection as well.

I attended many memorable roll calls in my life. One of the best was the day one of the chiefs retired and a lieutenant, always known for his practical jokes, hired a stripper to perform for the watch. Not content with just a regular strip-a-gram, he asked her to make her entrance into the squad room on a horse. However, I'd have to say that my all-time favorite roll call was the one in which I served everybody breakfast.

It all started with that asshole of a lieutenant who was

making my life a living hell because I wouldn't sleep with him. He had been riding me hard for weeks, complaining about every little thing I did that wasn't strictly by the book. My uniform had to be perfect every day. He told the sergeant to make me redo my paperwork if there was so much as a comma out of place. The morning before he had chewed me out royally for eating an orange in roll call.

"Hays, I don't see anyone *else* eating, do you?" he asked with a sneer. Actually I *did* see a lot of other people eating, but I didn't mention it at the time.

"Why is it that *you're* the only one who eats in roll call?" he went on. "What would we do if *everyone* decided to eat breakfast in roll call?"

I thought it was an interesting question.

The next morning I arrived bright and early with fresh-squeezed orange juice, bacon, blueberry waffles with whipped cream and strawberry jam, and coffee for twenty.

The guys loved their breakfast, but the lieutenant was not amused. He hollered at me in front of everyone for about ten minutes.

And he didn't even *touch* his breakfast.

RAPES AND RAPISTS

Victims of sexual assault shall be transported to an appropriate contract hospital for medical care and the collection of related medical evidence as soon as possible after the crime.

—FROM THE 1989 LAPD FIELD MANUAL (RULE 210.35)

There's a Mexican restaurant out near where I live that I used to go to all the time back in the mid-seventies. Lots of cops hung out there, because the margaritas were great, and they made the best, cheapest salsa and chicken burritos in these parts. Several years ago I suddenly stopped going in there. My friends couldn't figure out why the place didn't appeal to me anymore, but I never gave them a reason. I just didn't feel like telling people that the owner tried to rape me.

I like to think of myself as a savvy, street-smart woman, and when I'm working, that's just what I am. Sometimes, though, when I'm off duty, I let my guard down and become too trusting. Certainly I was naive that night in the Mexican restaurant.

I was there with a bunch of my police friends having a celebratory dinner—someone had just gone up in rank—and at some point late in the evening I walked down the hall toward the ladies' room. When I was on my way back to the table, the owner was waiting for me in the dim hallway. I had no idea what was coming when he waylaid me. I'd talked to him casually over the years, but he always seemed particularly shy and withdrawn to me. I was stunned when he grabbed me and gave me a passionate kiss. He was a good-looking guy, and frankly it was a great kiss, so I didn't worry about it. Figuring that it was just a one-shot deal, all I did was say something vaguely discouraging to him and rejoin my friends.

We were the last table of people to leave the restaurant that night, and as I walked to my car, in the far corner of the parking lot, the owner came up to me again. "I'll walk you to your car," he said, and I innocently let him.

On the way to my little car we had to pass the owner's trailer, which he kept in the lot so that he'd have a place to crash if he needed it. Just as we came alongside the trailer, he grabbed me and kissed me again. This time the kiss wasn't so nice, and it was only the beginning of what he had in mind. He ripped my clothes, a cotton jumpsuit with buttons down the front, as if it were made of so much tissue paper. Seconds later I was fighting him off in my bra and panties.

I made a move to run, but he held on to me, digging his

beefy fingers into my arm. I could tell that I was no match for him, especially since I didn't have my gun. Terrified, I kept struggling, but nothing did any good. He was mean and drunk and, at six feet and about 280 pounds, far too strong for me. I felt like a used toothpick. He threw me down on the ground and started to hump me, grinding on top of me through my underwear, right there in that deserted parking lot.

I couldn't believe what was happening to me. When I was a child, I promised myself that when I became an adult, no one would hurt me like this again. Then, when I became a cop, I knew I'd be okay. I would protect other people, and I would certainly be able to take care of myself. But then, believing that my badge would protect me, I had let my guard down. I felt like a fool.

He had his hand over my mouth, but I pulled it away and tried to reason with him. Since I couldn't overpower him, I thought if I could remind him that I was a *real* person, someone he *knew*, not some faceless, nameless thing, I could appeal to his senses and get him to change his mind.

"Will, this is Gayleen, your friend," I said urgently. "You know me. Don't do this. If you do this, I will never, ever forgive you. You are doing this to a *friend*."

My strategy worked. He quietly panted in my ear and stopped rubbing up against me. I lay there, not daring to breathe until he rolled over, his back facing me. He hadn't penetrated me—I still had my panties on—and I slowly, cautiously crawled away from him. I gathered up my clothes, kept backing toward my car, and managed to get in and drive back to the tiny apartment I shared with my girlfriend Josephine. She held me as I sobbed.

I could have prosecuted. I *should* have prosecuted. God knows that's what I had been telling victims to do ever since I had become a cop. But my old childhood feeling—that somehow it was my fault—resurfaced. Did I want revenge? Yes. You're damn straight. And it would have been easy to obtain considering what I did for a living. In the end, though, I decided to do what was best for me. On the one hand, I was embarrassed about having been so careless. On the other, I wasn't sure I was strong enough to face the questions and stares from my fellow officers. I knew I would feel deep humiliation during the interrogation, which would be conducted by friends of mine. I could not allow myself to be treated as a victim, not at work. It was too close to home. So, hating my decision, I kept quiet. I took a big step backward.

All women have to be aware of the possibility of rape. We know that we live in a world in which we can be victimized anytime, anyplace, and the realization that we have to be careful, on our guard, always lingers somewhere in the back of our minds. For a woman on the police force that knowledge stays at the *front* of her mind. For cops, rape is a fact of life.

According to the Field Manual, a rape case may be handled by both men and women police officers, but whenever a rape victim requests a female cop to talk to, she is entitled to have one. When first interviewing a rape victim, a male cop asks if she'd be more comfortable talking to a woman.

(Guys never have any trouble remembering to do this, because most of them aren't all that thrilled to deal with rape cases.)

In my twenty years I must have interviewed a couple of hundred rape victims. I suppose most women on the force have, since there weren't all that many of us to go around. No matter where I was working or how deeply asleep I was at the time, when a rape went down I could get called in to take the victim's statement. I've jumped out of bed more times than I care to count and driven halfway across the city to talk to some poor woman who has just been raped.

Like children who have been abused, rape victims break my heart. When I sat down with a woman who had just been raped and tried to get her to talk about it, it was torture for me to keep my objective, professional attitude. But I had to, for the sake of the victim. My showing emotion—whether anger or deep sympathy or horror—might cause her to become embarrassed or intimidated, and that might make her refuse to talk. What she really needed, although she might not think so, was to put into words the terrible experience she had just had. If she could tell someone else about it, she would be taking the first important step toward recovering from it. That's why my job was so critical and why I didn't really mind being dragged out of bed in the middle of the night.

Sometimes it would take awhile to get a victim to talk, especially if she was in shock or badly hurt. The first thing I did was take her to a doctor, to get her any treatment she needed and to collect the evidence we had to have to prove that a rape had taken place. I would usually stay in the examination room with the woman and talk her through it. Sometimes a social worker would be in there with us as well. Los Angeles has all kinds of resources for helping rape victims, including a twenty-four-hour rape hotline. There were volunteers who would come in at any time of the day or night and stay with a victim until she was feeling well enough to cope on her own.

One of the hardest things about any rape case is collecting evidence. Some women who have been violated jump right in the shower and try to scrub the filth away with soap and water. Many of them douche. I've seen a couple of women who shaved off their pubic hair after being raped. That reaction is perfectly understandable (the first thing I did after the night at the Mexican restaurant was to take a scalding hot shower and throw away my underwear), but it couldn't be more counterproductive as far as police work is concerned. To convict a rapist we need to keep everything the rapist touched, and that means sheets, underwear, and the victim herself, unscrubbed and unshaven.

In their distress, I've seen rape victims completely destroy a crime scene. Once when I answered a rape call, I found that the victim had taken everything—clothes, sheets, even the rug in her bedroom—and burned it all to a crisp in her fireplace. My heart went out to the poor woman, but I couldn't help feeling frustrated by what she had done. She didn't leave us much to go on.

After years of hearing about rapes and tracking down rapists I've just about seen it all. I've seen the bodies of hitchhikers who have been raped and cut to pieces, their body parts stuffed into plastic bags and left by the side of the road. I've also seen women who fought back. I'll never forget one prostitute who was about to be attacked by a rapist. She was a fast talker, and I guess he wasn't a rocket scientist, because she managed to persuade her attacker out of raping her and into letting her give him the best blow job he'd ever had. When he agreed, she bit his penis so hard she nearly took it off. She ran away and reported him. When he checked into a hospital, we nailed him—or I should say what was left of him.

I've heard of doctors who'd rape their patients and then charge them for visits. One doctor, a general practitioner, had been molesting his patients, especially the young girls, for years. Apparently he didn't do anything unacceptable until a girl reached her teens. Then, under the guise of giving a girl her first vaginal examination, he would rape her.

According to what we learned later, he was very charming about the whole thing. When the girl was lying on the table with her feet in the stirrups, he would speak very softly and appear to be totally professional.

"Now I am just going to put my finger inside and make sure everything is healthy," he would say, only instead of using his finger, he used his cock. Finally, one of his patients, a smarter than average fifteen-year-old girl, got suspicious and looked to see what he was doing. (She told us later that "it sounded weird.") She told her mother, who had been taking all of her children to this doctor for twenty years, and her mother told us. When we investigated, we discovered that he had raped dozens of young female patients.

Another bizarre case involved a guy whose M.O. was to break into people's houses and hide under the bed until a man and woman had gone to bed. Sometimes he would lie on the floor for hours. Then, when both of them had gone deeply to sleep, he would crawl over to the woman's side of the bed and wake her up very gently with his gun. The gun and his whispered threats were usually enough to intimidate her into letting him have sex with her. The husband almost never woke up, but if he did, he was threatened too. When the rapist was finished, he would gag and tie up the woman and take off into the night. When she woke the man up, it would be too late for him to do anything.

Unfortunately for the rapist, one night his knots didn't do the trick. His victim worked herself free and called us in time for us to follow his trail. We didn't get the pleasure of taking him to trial, however. In the high-speed chase that followed he wrapped his car around a telephone pole and died instantly.

Another really strange rapist I remember drove along a busy street and stopped next to a woman who was carrying a huge sack of laundry, obviously on her way to the laundromat about a block away. He pulled up next to the woman and asked her a question in a voice so low she had to get closer to hear him. When she leaned toward him, he pointed his gun at her and told her to get in. She said later that she probably should have made a run for it—there were plenty of people around—but she was too surprised and frightened at the time. She dropped her laundry in the middle of the sidewalk and got in the car.

Keeping his gun pointed at the woman, the man headed for the freeway and started driving really fast. When he got up to about seventy miles per hour, he unzipped his fly, took out his cock, and told the woman to give him a blow job. The faster she got him off, he said, the faster she could get back to her laundry.

He was true to his word. Fifteen minutes later she was back on the spot where the nightmare had begun. The sack of laundry was right where she left it.

I KNOW THERE'S a lot of irresponsible talk about why some people are raped and even more ignorant talk about women who "ask for it." The idea that any woman wants or deserves to be violated in that way is asinine and not even worthy of discussion. Being the victim of a rape has nothing whatsoever to do with what you look like, how you're dressed, or how old you are. It has everything to do with what is in the sick, twisted mind of the rapist.

I have seldom met a rape victim who looked or acted provocative in any way. Women can be out there in a dirty, baggy sweatsuit, and believe me, if someone comes along who thinks she's the woman of his dreams, she's in big trouble. If I learned anything from my experience covering rapes, it's that we can't comprehend what rapists fantasize about or what makes them do what they do. Some consider rape a sex crime; others say it's about violence and power, not sex. I'd say it's a mixed bag, and probably a lot of other things as well. I have noticed one consistent detail: Most women who have been raped describe their rapist's penis as unusually small.

We once busted a twenty-two-year-old who had been climbing into the windows of apartment houses where little old ladies lived and raping them. Some of the women were in their eighties. Many of them didn't hear well enough even to know that there was an intruder in the house, and none of them was strong enough to resist. He raped some of them in their sleep. What, I wonder, was the motivation there?

We've had rapists who fall "in love" with their victims, or at least their version of love. In some kind of grotesque courtship ritual a rapist like that will track down his victim when he gets out of prison and rape her again. (There's no law that says we have to inform victims when their rapists are released from prison, but we always did our best to let people know.)

One of the strangest cases I ever worked on was what a bunch of us called the Case of the Remorseful Rapist. One night we caught a burglar in the act of methodically cleaning out a small house, and we took him in for interrogation. He must have been a little strung out at the time, because as soon as we asked him the first question, the floodgates opened. He didn't just tell us about the burglaries, though. He assumed we knew that he had also committed some rapes—eighteen of them, to be exact, and all within the last six months. He confessed to them all and said he was as sorry as he could be.

He was so sorry, in fact, that he volunteered to drive

around with us in one of our unmarked cars and point out the scenes of his many crimes and tell us exactly what happened inside and when. The guy was a young, good-looking body-builder type, quite charming in a way, and he'd been working door-to-door all over the city. Sometimes he would pose as a researcher taking a market survey. Other times he would pretend to sell pots and pans or distribute free samples of a household cleaning product. Whenever he found a woman he liked, he would talk his way into her house and rape her.

Afterward he would hug the woman and cry. "I've never done anything like this before in my life," he'd say. "But you're so beautiful and sexy I just couldn't help myself. I am so terribly sorry. I hope you can forgive me."

Damned if it didn't work. I guess they did feel sorry for him. Not *one* of his victims lodged a complaint or reported a rape. And after he confessed his crimes to us, only two of the eighteen housewives would admit to having been raped and press charges against the guy. The rest would not even acknowledge that he had raped them.

When it comes to rape, you can never underestimate the power of the intimidation factor. Rapists never do; they know very well that many women are just too damn scared to report a rape. That's what a guy we arrested a few years ago was counting on. And his plan would have worked except for one thing: The victim was more afraid of her boyfriend than she was of the asshole who raped her.

As the story was told to us, this lovely nineteen-year-old girl who worked as a cleaning woman got a call one day from her boyfriend's best friend and fellow gang member. His apartment was a mess, he said, and he wanted to hire her to clean it.

The young woman checked with her extremely jealous and possessive boyfriend to see if it was all right, and he agreed to let her do it. When she arrived at the friend's apartment with her cleaning products that morning, the friend was still sleeping. He woke up long enough to let her in and told her that he'd been up all night and needed some more rest. Would she please save the bedroom until last? he asked. She agreed.

She cleaned all morning. Finally, all that was left was the bedroom. At about noon she knocked on the bedroom door and said softly: "Are you ready for me to clean in there?"

"Yes, come on in," he answered.

When she walked into the room, he was waiting for her with a knife. He slammed the bedroom door behind her and locked it. Then, still holding the knife to her throat, he raped her over and over and over again—fifteen times in three hours, according to the young woman's story. He said he would kill her if she made a sound. After it was over, he told her to get the hell out of the apartment. And, he added, she'd better not think of telling her boyfriend about what had happened. He'd never believe a word of it.

The truth is, she *was* afraid to tell her boyfriend, but the fear of his finding out that she had had sex with someone else was even greater. She decided to take her chances and tell her boyfriend the truth about his so-called friend. It was her boyfriend who brought her into the station to press charges. I always suspected that he was counting on us to see if she was telling the truth. Her story was a little hard to take, but when we saw the scene of the crime we believed every word. There was semen everywhere, and we found the knife, too.

I met a lot of very brave women when I worked on rape cases, but the bravest, and perhaps craziest, I ever saw was a realtor I met about four years ago. One late afternoon she came out of a supermarket, pushing her things in a shopping cart, and a young man approached her.

"Can I help you with those?"

(For the record, rapists normally ask what time it is, so that you'll look away from them and at your watch.)

"Oh, thank you," she replied. "They are a little heavy."

When they got to her car, he helped her unload the groceries and then pulled a gun on her. After getting in the car with her, he told her to drive up into the hills. When they got there, he picked a secluded spot and raped her. His thing was anal sex. He made her bend over the hood of her car and sodomized her.

The woman was terrified and in pain, but she didn't scream or cry out or struggle. When he was finished and they were driving back down into the city, she decided to set a trap for him.

"That was fantastic," she told the guy. "You're wonderful, much better than my boring husband. We've been married for twenty years, and I've never had sex like this in my life. Call me whenever you get horny."

And she actually gave him her business card.

The moment she was free, she called us and told us what

had happened. We had already heard about this guy. It wasn't the first time he'd kidnapped a woman from that area and raped her up in the hills. We knew that he drove a motorcycle, and we suspected that he was gay. But we didn't have a very good description of him, and we weren't even close to nailing him. When we heard what this woman had done, we went through the motions of being horrified. How could she have further endangered herself by giving him her number? we asked sternly. Who did she think she was, a cop? Off the record, however, we were hoping that her crazy move might lead to something. We agreed that if he did call, I'd keep the date.

He called. Just as we had rehearsed, she told him she was busy but she had a girlfriend he'd go for in a big way. She gave him a description of me and said that he was just my type. We met, she identified him from an unmarked car, and we arrested his ass. Thank God rapists are sometimes as stupid as they are mean. That was one of the most satisfying arrests I was ever involved with.

THE FIRST FALSE rape report I ever took was when I was very new on the job, back when I had a greater tendency than I do now to believe everything I was told. I was working the desk, and into the station marched this gay woman, accompanied by her lover, and she claimed that a bunch of men had raped her. There were four of them, she explained, and they had forced her into their car, gang raped her, and kept her out all night.

I listened sympathetically and then took her to the hospital for an examination, where I was told that there was no evidence that anyone's penis had been anywhere near her vagina for a long, long time.

Still, she stuck to her story, and I believed her. I actually drove her all around the neighborhood looking for the guys and for their car. We were out for hours, but we didn't have any luck.

By the time I got back to the station, the guys were in hysterics about what I had been through. They knew I was being set up, and they knew that I didn't know, because I was so wet behind the ears. An experienced cop would have been able to scope out the scene within seconds. The woman was lying to cover up something that she didn't want her lover to know, and a rape was the only thing she could come up with to explain her overnight absence. (It turned out that she was supposed to come home straight from work, but instead she had a couple of drinks and then spent the night with a cocktail waitress.)

Today I'd know she was lying, and I'd do it all differently. I'd take down her statement, ask her to sign it, and then decide which detective I'm not too crazy about at the moment. Then I'd give the victim a receipt and tell her, "I've taken the report, as you can see. Now be sure to call Detective So-and-So, because he'll be doing the follow-up on this." That way I could kill two birds with one stone: get rid of the lying victim and enjoy a chuckle, having passed her on to some other unsuspecting cop.

I once had a partner over in West Valley who was really great at getting rid of liars and crackpots. Victor would listen for a while, and then, finally out of patience, he'd turn on the person. "All right, I've had enough of this bullshit. You're boring me now," he'd say. "It was okay when you were interesting, but now I'm sick of listening to you." Then came the finale: "All right! Everybody out! Everybody out of my station!" I never saw his system fail. The crackpots always left without a peep.

I took more than a few false rape reports in my time, and they were almost always like that, a cover-up for the truth. Apparently it was easier for some women to claim to have been abducted and raped than to admit to screwing around on their husbands, for instance. Many a cokehead came into the station crying rape when what really happened was she stayed out all night partying with her pals. Now her father or husband or boyfriend would be wondering where the hell she'd been all night, and her first thought was to turn to us with a rape report.

I used to wonder what ever happened to "I lost my keys" or "I fell asleep and lost track of the time." I guess no one is naive enough to buy those alibis anymore.

O NE OF THE most horrifying truths about rapists is that they don't usually do it just once. A guy who rapes one woman is extremely likely to rape another, and usually in the same way. Most rapists have patterns they like to follow, in the kinds of victims they choose, the surroundings they prefer, and the weapons they use. The only good news in all this is that their tendency to repeat themselves makes them easier to catch.

About five years ago there was a rapist at large in the

Topanga Canyon Mall for a few weeks. It was wintertime, and he liked to strike at around dusk. At about five-thirty in the evening he would go to the mall and cruise the parking lot, waiting for women who had finished their shopping and were heading, bags in hand, back to their cars. Then he'd strike up a conversation with them, walk them to their cars, help them with their bags, and force them into their own backseats and rape them at gunpoint. He always got away, but several of the victims were able to identify him: tall, handsome, blond, athletic-looking, wearing very dark sunglasses.

When the detectives asked to use me as a decoy to get this guy, I jumped at the chance. We got me the perfect undercover car, an old Chevy with a great big backseat, and I went out one evening and shopped my way through the mall, accompanied by a small army of backups. Someone spotted him right away, and when I got the signal that he was there, I made sure he spotted me. I had a ton of packages, and I made all kinds of noises as I maneuvered my shopping cart out of the building and toward my car.

"Hi," I heard a man say.

I turned around and saw our suspect. Sometimes being a cop is wonderful. I couldn't wait to nail this asshole.

"Hi," I answered. "Can you believe how much stuff I have? Look at all this junk."

"I hope my girlfriend hasn't bought that much. I'm supposed to meet her out here in ten minutes," he said. Several of his earlier victims had said he talked about a girlfriend.

As we were talking, he began to walk with me, very casually.

"You look as if you could use some help unloading this stuff," he said. Again, that's what he'd been saying to the others.

He followed me to my car and helped me load the trunk. Then, as I opened the door, I could see him reaching into his pocket.

I immediately pretended to trip and fell to the ground. On my way down, I grabbed his foot and yanked him down with me, pulling out my own gun at the same time. Within moments, my backup arrived, and they took him off to jail. Case closed.

Just a few months before I left the job there was a series of horrible attacks in Sepulveda Park. Women running along the jogging path in the very early morning—five, four, or even three o'clock sometimes—were being brutally raped. When I read the first report of what was going on, I knew I wanted to work the case. The guy came at the victim from behind, smashed her across the back of the head with a board or a big stick, dragged her by her hair through the mud, raped her, and left her for dead. The victims were discovered by other joggers.

The first time it happened we all thought: "Okay, it's some horny transient. He might not do it again." But then he did. Neither of the first two women could give us a description; after all, he had come at them from behind and knocked them unconscious before he raped them. The third victim got a bit of a look at him. He was short—about five three, she said—and had lots of gold teeth.

There were four rapes over a period of a couple of months, and it finally hit the papers, with much debate

about how any woman in her right mind could be out
running in the middle of the night. What did these women
expect when they behaved so foolishly? Others responded
with equal outrage: by God, those women have a right to be
anywhere they want at any hour. If they want to go running
at three in the morning, they ought to be able to do so in
safety.

As far as I'm concerned, that argument is a complete
waste of time. Both sides are right—those women *were* nuts
and they had every right to *be* nuts—and both were completely beside the point. I wasn't the least bit interested in
debating the issue. What I wanted to do was nail the bastard
who was doing it. That was exactly the kind of crime that
got my hunter's instincts going. After the third rape, I
started in on poor Lieutenant Pooler, begging him to use me
as a decoy and let me get a crack at the guy. The captain and
the lieutenant finally agreed. I was going out for some exercise at four o'clock in the morning. I'd wear a wire in my
bra and have plenty of backup. We were going to get this
guy.

We decided that I would walk instead of run, so my little
pug dog was enlisted to go undercover as well. My daughter
Serina helped me with my costume: she took a pair of
scissors and cut up my white sweatshirt so that it was nothing but fringe, and I wore hot pink bicycle pants. I left my
hair hanging down, very sloppy, and I carried my gun in an
old baggy-looking purse. I wanted to look a little flaky, like
someone who didn't quite have her act together. My specialty. There was a heavy ground fog that early in the morn-

ing and no moon at all. It was pitch dark when I arrived there. On one side of the path were the mud flats, and on the other was a golf course. A bunch of our guys were wearing combat fatigues and hiding in the bushes or behind rocks.

I was the only woman out there, because we had blocked off the path and were letting only men come through. There were no police cars in the area and no helicopters, on express orders from the captain. When I had been walking for about a half hour, the fog was starting to lift, but it was still pretty hazy. All of a sudden I heard somebody come up behind me. I glanced back quickly and saw that it was a man and that he was on the short side, but I couldn't tell much more than that. (I didn't see any gold teeth.) I *could* tell that he was watching me.

My dog and I went into our act.

"Aw, Tara," I said to her, "you're so cute. Oh, you wanna go over to those bushes?"

We walked over to the bushes, strolled around them, and came out the other side. The guy watched me the whole time, but he kept his distance. He didn't pick up a weapon.

I tried again when we came to a large rock a few minutes later.

"Tara, look at the rock. Come with Mommy and we'll see what's behind the rock."

He stayed behind me, getting quite close—I could see the gold teeth now—but he still didn't approach me or pick up a weapon.

It pains me terribly to write these words, but he never did make a move toward me that night, so we never got exactly what we came for. When we had been out there for almost an hour, he finally passed me on the path and began to walk away. We arrested him anyway, because we had probable cause. He was a short transient with gold teeth, and he was on the Sepulveda Park jogging path at four in the morning. That was good enough for us even if it might not be good enough for a conviction. (It wasn't.)

Still, the story had a moderately happy ending. After that night, when we scared the shit out of that guy, the rapes stopped. We probably got our bad guy after all.

13

THE HOME
FRONT

The nature of the law enforcement task requires
Department employees to have the ability to work
irregular duty schedules which are subject to
change in meeting deployment needs.

—FROM THE 1989 LAPD FIELD MANUAL
(RULE 270.30)

My husband, Mark, has always been an incredible romantic. Before we were married, his idea of a perfect evening included wine, candlelight, soft music, and evenings by the fire. (It still does, I'm glad to say.) One night, several months after we started going out together, I had been on night watch for nearly a month and we hadn't any time together to speak of. Mark said he wanted to celebrate my day off by cooking a beautiful dinner for me at my place. We would spend a romantic evening alone together and make love all night long. I couldn't imagine anything more wonderful, and I readily agreed to his plan.

At about eleven o'clock that night we had finished our wonderful dinner and were just enjoying the last sips of our Chardonnay with some cheese and fresh grapes when the phone rang. My heart sank, along with a few other parts of my body. When an off-duty cop's phone rings late at night, it's almost never good news.

It was my thirteen-year-old stepdaughter, and she needed help. (When my second husband and I separated, I didn't stop loving his kids.) Sobbing into the phone, she told me what had happened. "I'm all by myself in this house, I just called the police, but no one's come yet. I'm scared! I don't know what to do," she wailed.

I calmed her down and told her she'd have to be more specific.

"There's a man outside my window, and he's looking in."

That's all I needed to hear. "I'll be right there," I said. I turned to Mark and said, "I'll be right back."

I grabbed my badge and my gun and dashed out the door. Mark was right behind me. "You're not going anywhere without me," he said. I didn't want him tagging along, but I didn't have time to argue.

We jumped into my little car and screamed up the street to my stepdaughter's house, just a few blocks away. On the way I was saying, "Mark, I don't want you to get hurt. There's a suspect out there, and you're not trained for this. When we get there, just stay in the car." He said he'd do as I asked.

I hadn't been to roll call that day, so I didn't know that the cops already knew about the guy my stepdaughter had seen. The guy was a real psycho; he'd been raping women and then, as a finishing touch, taking a crap in their yards afterward. He had done it four times in the area already. There was a special unit assigned to his case. Of course, I didn't know any of this at the time.

When we got to my stepdaughter's house, there was certainly no unit that I could see. Again I told Mark to stay in the car, and I got out to take a look around. I spotted the suspect right away, looking in my stepdaughter's bedroom window. He was young, maybe twenty years old, and on the small side, about five nine, 140 pounds. I knew I had a crime—he was trespassing—so I got ready to arrest him. I didn't want to wait. I might lose him.

I walked up behind him and said the magic words.

"Freeze, asshole. Police. You're under arrest. Stay where you are and put your hands above your head."

I pulled back my shirt to reveal my badge. My other hand rested on my gun.

He wasn't impressed. As I recall, his exact words were, *"Fuck you, bitch. Shoot me."*

Then he turned around and ran up the block. I started after him, but he was *fast*. Normally I'm pretty speedy too, but I had dropped a bottle of champagne on my foot the day before, and that slowed me down. I wasn't going to be able to catch him. That's when Mark decided to get involved. He didn't know what had gone on so far, and he had no way of knowing that we were dealing with a real bad guy here. All he knew was that some puny little guy was running away, and his girlfriend probably wasn't going to be able to catch him. Mark, who's big, strong, and unafraid—and also pretty fast on his feet—wanted to help. He took off after the guy.

He caught him a couple of blocks away and nailed him near a tree in somebody's front yard. As I ran toward them, Mark pinned him against the tree, and the puny guy I was still thinking of as a simple trespasser began to plead for mercy.

"Please, mister, I didn't do anything," he whimpered. "I wasn't doing anything. Let me go, please."

Mark said, "If you didn't do anything, nothing will happen to you. So let's just wait until the police get here. You can tell them all about it."

The guy kept struggling, so Mark threw him on the ground and pinned him. I was only thirty yards away by then.

The guy started whimpering again. "Oh, please let me go, mister. I didn't do anything. You're holding me too tight. I can't breathe."

Mark loosened his grip just a little, and the guy jumped at his chance. He tore his right arm loose and pulled a gun from underneath his waistband. Mark caught his arm coming up but the momentum carried the gun to his neck. The kid pulled the trigger. I got there, with my own gun drawn, just in time to hear that horrible click. Mark says that he still hears that click in his dreams.

When Mark realized that he wasn't dead, he grabbed the gun away from the kid. That's when I took over. I didn't shoot the guy. Once he'd been disarmed, I knew I didn't have to shoot. Besides, I didn't want Mark to have to see me shoot somebody. There's a lot of noise and mess and trauma connected to a shooting, and I thought he'd gone through more than enough already. Believe me, it took a lot of self-control. The moment I heard that click and saw Mark's face, it would have been a pleasure to blow the guy away.

That night, as I watched Mark grow more quiet, I knew he was going through the typical stage anyone does when he's almost been killed. "For a while, you are going to feel very close to me because we've been through something very traumatic together," I said, stroking his head. "Also," I warned, stroking his neck where the asshole's gun had pushed against his skin, "you're going to hear the click of that gun in the middle of the night, in your dreams, in your silences, for a long, long time. But that will pass. Just give yourself time."

Mark sat quietly as I talked, but I noticed the subtle messages in his eyes. My words had hit their target. Finally, he smiled weakly and said, "You've got a couple more days off. Let's go to the mountains and get the hell outta here."

"I'll be ready in five minutes," I promised.

"There's just one thing I don't want you to forget to pack . . ." he said.

"What's that?" I asked.

"Your gun," he said, and he smiled.

The guy was eventually brought to trial for rape. During the trial one of the victims who had seen me in court walked over to me and said, "You should have killed that bastard when you had the chance."

NO ONE WAS more surprised than Mark when he married a cop. Like a lot of people who went to college in Madison, Wisconsin, in the late sixties, Mark has never been all that enchanted with cops. As he tells it, he never actually hollered "pig" at anyone, but he thought about it, a lot. He certainly never dreamed he'd actually end up married to one.

It hasn't always been easy, either. I've said before that cops are most comfortable when they're with their own kind, and I know that my family has felt left out some of the time when I'm caught up in my work. The stress of the job has definitely made it more challenging than it might have been; coping with my crazy month in COBRA, some of my scarier undercover work, and the more horrendous child abuse cases has been tough for both of us. We had our arguments, especially in the early days of the marriage, but we got through it.

I can't say we've had much of a normal social life either. I don't suppose any cop does. For one thing cops cannot and will not stay at any party where drugs are being used; I can't tell you how many social events I've gone to for ten minutes and then had to make an excuse to leave. Even when Mark and I did socialize, I think there were many people who just weren't comfortable having a cop around. Everybody gets a little uptight in the company of police officers. After all, they're *not* regular people. They're cops.

Cops always say that we drop the job as soon as the badge goes on the dresser, but that was never true for me and I don't think it was for anybody else either. Cops are on duty twenty-four hours a day, and that's the kind of preoccupation that can ruin marriages.

Mark and I never talked much about the danger, although I'm sure it was brought home to him quite clearly the night he heard the click of a gun in his ear. We had a kind of truce. I didn't nag Mark about his parachute jumping and his hang gliding and his hot-air ballooning, and he didn't nag me about the dangers of police work. He trusts my judgment and my ability to do things, and I trust his. Maybe that's the secret: cops should always marry daredevils.

Sometimes I think that the greatest danger to cops has nothing whatsoever to do with getting shot. What will probably kill most cops in the end is sitting around in an undercover car smoking cigarettes, eating junk food, and drinking after work. Smoking is supposedly very much out of fashion now, especially out here in fitness-obsessed Los Angeles—but I guess the news hasn't quite caught up with the LAPD. Not everyone on the force smokes cigarettes, but many do, and there wasn't much that those of us who didn't could do about avoiding their secondhand smoke. On my last job my sergeant and lieutenant were both chain-smokers, so I didn't see much point in telling them I couldn't breathe.

Once I did make a passing comment to the sergeant—"It sure would be nice if we had a designated smoking area, don't you think, Sergeant?" He responded by blowing smoke in my face. I took that for a no.

Food was another problem. I had to watch the revolting stuff that the guys ate day after day, but I didn't actually have to eat it myself. The real problem was, I really *like* some food that isn't all that great for me, and the guys all knew it. Night after night on surveillance or in the station, I'd sit there nibbling on my baked potato or my fresh fruit and give them a really hard time about their cholesterol- and fat-filled pizza slices and french fries. Eventually they'd get sick and tired of listening to me and get their revenge. One night I'd get into my car or walk over to my desk, and there would be all my favorite foods lined up for my dining pleasure: ice cream, onion rings, chunky peanut butter, and chocolates. So much for my baked potato.

I've never had any problem going for eight or more hours without eating, so for most of my years on the job I didn't take a meal break. When everyone else went to Code 7, I'd use the time to work out—sometimes I'd walk up and down the stairs for a half hour—or at least walk around and get some air. Police work is wonderful, but it sure doesn't keep you fit.

I've always thought that a police officer's badge should come with a warning: CAUTION: SHIFT WORK MAY BE HAZARD- OUS TO YOUR MARRIAGE. The reason is obvious: while the rest of the world, including your spouse and kids, is having a nine-to-five life, shift workers are in a time warp all their own. It's especially hard on cops because they usually have rotating shifts; every three months they make a switch. Just when they're getting used to staying up all night and sleep- ing during the day, they have to get used to getting their sleep in the late afternoon. And their families have to get used to it too.

I'll never forget this poor woman I worked with in the jail. She had been happily married for about eight years, and she loved her husband to death. They had two adorable little girls. She used to talk all the time about how wonderful their sex life was and how happy they were. One day she changed shifts—from nights to days—and apparently her husband forgot about it. She went home at the end of her new shift and found her husband in bed with one of their neighbors.

Every shift has its good and bad points. With the day shift (seven to three) you get to live a relatively normal life as far as the rest of the world is concerned, but you end up completely snowed under in paperwork, not to mention interfering brass who live to second-guess everything you do. When you work the P.M. watch (three to midnight), you usually end up drinking too much. You get off work, and you're not ready to go to bed yet. There's not much else to do when the rest of the world is asleep except go to a bar or go home and drink to get sleepy. A lot of people on the job drink heavily.

To me the worst shift of all was seven at night until three in the morning. With that shift it was impossible to have any kind of a normal life. It ruined the morning, the day, and the night. I always liked the morning shift (midnight to eight in the morning) the best—lots of action, not too much paperwork, and no brass in sight—until that terrible moment when I had to walk out into the sunlight. It would give me a headache almost every time. I wasn't the only one who found it tough to adjust to the daylight after working all night. One female officer on the force almost got killed driving home with the sun in her eyes. She had worked nine days in a row, and she had a long drive, all the way to Canyon Country. On the way she got into a terrible accident and spent several weeks in the hospital.

"On the wheel" is an expression that cops use when they first join the force. When a cop is "on the wheel," he's on probation, and he has to be assigned to six different places in a year. It's all part of the learning process. Every couple of months he moves to another spot and learns the ropes there. The idea is that when the wheel stops spinning, he'll have accumulated many different kinds of experience. In some ways that wheel never stops spinning for police officers, with their rotating shifts and strange schedules. But I always liked that. And so do a lot of cops I've worked with.

A cop's work calendar isn't measured off in months; we have deployment periods. A deployment period is a lot like a month; it's a four-week stint in which we get nine days off (in the deployment period that includes Christmas we get ten days off) and work nineteen. We never know in advance which days will be which; it's completely up to the discretion, not to mention the whim and the lousy mood, of the lieutenant or sergeant in charge. Technically, you can't work all nineteen days in a row, but if the department needs you, that's exactly what you have to do.

The way the system works is that the assignment sheet is passed around, and everyone has a chance to circle the nine days off he or she would like in the next deployment period. (The only stipulation is that everyone who wants one is entitled to one Sunday off.) The sergeant takes it from there and coordinates the schedules.

As you can probably imagine, some of the hotshots in charge of making assignments would occasionally abuse their power or let it go to their heads. (I don't think I've ever met a woman on the force who didn't, at least once, have a sergeant offer her a Saturday off in return for a quickie in the back room.) And they can be pretty erratic in their thinking. One lieutenant up and decided one day that the whole bunch of us were getting too set in our ways. We'd been on the same schedule too long, and we were starting to get too attached to one another. It was time to shake things up, he decreed, and he told the sergeant to change everybody's schedule. It's an unwritten rule in the police force: never let the brass know that you love your job or your shift or your partner, because they'll find some way to change it. They have that power.

For the first ten years of my life on the job, before my daughter was born, there was no such thing as a weekend or a holiday. Now that I look back on it, I think I was a bit of a martyr then. I was so excited to be a cop that I automatically took the worst shifts. I took days so that the *real* cops could have weekends off. Then I discovered there was a lot more action on weekends, especially Friday nights. The only day I refused to work was April Fools' Day, which is also my birthday.

Working holidays was a mixed bag. On the one hand, I

missed spending them with family and friends; on the other hand, there tended to be a lot more action on weekends and holidays. I regarded holidays as a challenge, too. I knew that if I used my ingenuity, I could find some way to celebrate and have some fun. One Thanksgiving I took up a collection and I cooked a great big twenty-five-pound turkey, complete with stuffing, in the jail oven. Believe it or not, it tasted great, and everybody seemed to appreciate it. The next Thanksgiving I was on night watch, and I brought in pumpkin pie for everyone in the jail. The pie didn't go over quite as well as the bird. As I recall, a couple of the prisoners threw theirs at me. (My friends told me pecan pie would have been the better choice.) One Christmas I hung a wreath over the cage and wrapped tinsel around the buttons of my uniform shirt.

Halloween was never a disappointing time to be on duty. That's the night when the weird get weirder. When I was working the desk at night, after the brass had gone home and the trick-or-treaters came out, I would put on a fabulous monkey mask that fit perfectly with my policewoman uniform, and I gave my partner, Victor, a gorilla face to go with it. We made quite a pair.

As far back as I can remember, I always worked on New Year's Eve, a strange night in any police station. One of the strangest I can remember was a night about twelve years ago. I started my shift at midnight, and when I got there, I saw a man and woman sitting on the bench in the lobby. I couldn't tell at first if they were a couple. They were both talking nonstop, very quietly, but they didn't seem to be talking to each other. Then I noticed that every once in a while one of them would touch the other, and there seemed to be some affection there. All around them people were making noise and wishing each other "Happy New Year," but the man and woman just stayed on the bench, in their own little world.

As the night wore on, I realized that both of them were street people with some mental problems. They had no business being in the station, but I couldn't bring myself to turn them out onto the street on New Year's Eve. Besides, I liked them. I was always having to throw drunks out of the station, but these people were different. By the end of my shift the three of us had become friends. I ended up buying them breakfast. After they finished enough pancakes to feed an army, I went to work to find a social agency to help them.

MY HUSBAND COMES from a fairly conservative background. In Mark's family, all of whom were raised and educated in Wisconsin, the men don't generally make it a habit to marry women in the police force. When his parents and his brothers and sisters were with us, I always kept a low profile about my work, and Mark agreed that that was wise. The less they knew about what I did, the less alarmed they would become. That was not a problem for me. I've never been one to make a big deal out of being a policewoman when I'm with family and friends.

My strategy worked pretty well, I think. After all, I didn't look much like what they think of as a cop, and I didn't act like one either, at least not at family weddings and anniversary parties. Then, just a few years ago, something happened to all of us that brought the truth home in a hurry. My in-laws were staying with us for a couple of weeks, spoiling their precious grandchild, and some time during their stay I came down with a bad cold and decided to stay home for the day.

I kept to my bed for a while, but I felt well enough to get up and sit around in my old bathrobe drinking tea in the late afternoon. Neither of Mark's parents felt comfortable about driving in the area, so at one point they asked if I'd mind taking them to a grocery store just a couple of miles away at El Camino Shopping Center. They were making dinner, and they needed to pick up a few crucial ingredients. Mark wasn't due home for a couple of hours.

I stayed in my bathrobe and drove them to the store. They had been inside for a few minutes when I became aware that something out of the ordinary was going on. A moment later I heard shots fired, and a huge plate glass window was shattered. I could see that the place was full of customers, including a couple of very nervous Wisconsinites, and I could also see that there was a guy inside with a great big gun.

The guy came running out of the store, and one of the idiots inside decided to chase him. The bad guy shot at his pursuer, and I could see that all hell was about to break loose. I looked at the guy's gun longingly, wishing that I'd had the foresight to carry one in my bathrobe. Still, even without a gun, I had to do something. I ran to the side door of the store and shouted some orders.

"Everybody get down on the floor and start crawling toward the back door," I instructed them. "Be sure to stay low and cover your heads."

I'm sure my voice had authority, but I don't think the bathrobe inspired much confidence in those people. My mother-in-law, bless her heart, came to my rescue.

"It's okay, everybody. This is my daughter, and she's a cop." Then she and my father-in-law led the shoppers out the back door to safety.

So much for keeping a low profile.

I'M NOT A particularly phobic person. I don't suppose anyone could be and do a good job as a cop. I like spiders and have had pet snakes. I'm not troubled by flying or heights. But I *am* afraid of the dark. Most of the time it doesn't bother me very much, but once in a while, especially when I'm home alone and very tired, I get a little squirrelly. There's something about the dark that brings back the day's work to me, especially child abuse cases, rapes, and burglaries in which some asshole breaks in while the lady of the house is sleeping.

I'm usually all right when my husband or even my daughter is home to keep me company, but when they're away, I'm a wreck. You wouldn't believe my bedtime ritual. I take forever to lock up—checking all the doors and windows at least twice—and then I spend another age trying to decide which lights I'm going to leave on. Once in a while I take myself in hand and decide I'm being silly; then I turn off all the lights and go to bed. Thirty seconds later—during which time my heart has been beating so loud I swear the neighbors must be able to hear it—I'm up and flipping switches again. (I'll take a real criminal over the one in my imagination every time.)

I admit that's pretty extraordinary behavior for a cop. I've tried giving myself stern lectures ("For God's sake, you're a grown-up, and a grown-up cop at that. There's nothing to be afraid of. If something *does* happen, which it won't, you can handle it"), but they don't do any good. Neither do pep talks from Mark and Serina, who are used to my night terror but will never understand it. They have no idea what it feels like to fear being attacked in your sleep.

One night about two years ago I was home alone, and I had gone to sleep, with just one little night-light on. I was pretty proud of myself for being so brave. At about one o'clock in the morning, just about the time I was sliding into a deep sleep, I heard a noise. My bedroom door, which I thought was closed, squeaked a little. I flew out of bed, grabbed my gun, and decided right then and there that whoever was there was about to become history. It had to be a bad guy, I thought. No one ever breaks into a house and goes into a bedroom to do something wonderful. I got up, turned on every light in the house, and checked every inch of the place.

Nothing.

I said to myself, "Now this is stupid. Just go back to bed and get some sleep. You're just imagining things."

I walked back into the bedroom, plumped the pillows, and started to get in. But I knew there was no way in the world that I was going to be sleeping in that bed. I grabbed my pillow, my blanket, and my gun and headed for my car, which was parked on the street in front of my house. The streetlights looked mighty inviting from where I stood, and I decided to spend the night in my own backseat. I figured, "It's one o'clock in the morning in front of my house. I'll be fine."

I locked myself in the car and got comfortable. Again, just as I was about to drift off, I was interrupted, this time by something flying through the air and hitting me in the chest. I had forgotten to close the back window, and the intruder had come in that way.

I drew my gun and flipped on the light. Fortunately, I didn't shoot. It was my cat.

PULLING
THE PIN

Police Officer Gayleen Hays toasts her retirement
with a limousine and a glass of bubbly outside
LAPD headquarters downtown. . . . She took early
retirement at 47 after spending 22 years on the
force. Hays borrowed her mother's black sequined
evening dress for the occasion.

—CAPTION, *LOS ANGELES TIMES*,
OCTOBER 14, 1989

As I've mentioned before, that famous burlesque
dancer Gay Dawn, also known as my mom,
used to say that an audience always remembers the first five
minutes and the last five minutes of your act. "Always give
them a great start and a knockout finish," she used to tell
me. On my first day as a policewoman I strolled into the Van
Nuys Jail dressed like a "fuckin' stewardess" and made a
complete jackass of myself. I decided that on my last day as
a policewoman I was going out in *style*.

I woke at six in the morning, took a nice long shower,

fluffed up my hair, and put on one of my mother's old stripper dresses. I still have quite a few of them tucked away, and it was hard to choose which one would have exactly the effect I was going for. In the end I went with basic black—a slinky, long, black sequined number slit up the back all the way to the knee. I added a pair of black spiked heels, applied a thin coat of lipstick, and splashed on a little of my favorite perfume. Finally, I jammed my gun and my handcuffs in my silver evening bag and grabbed my feather boa. Then, all ready for my last day of work, I waited for the limousine to pick me up. The limo was my husband's idea. ("Go ahead," Mark said. "Live it up. This is your last day on the job. You've got to remember it." If it had been *his* last day, I'm sure he would have parachuted out of a plane.)

As I waited for the limo, I realized that I was relaxed for the first time in a month. During that last deployment period I had found myself getting a little bit superstitious; I read somewhere that fighting soldiers are the same way, doubly worried about getting hurt once they have orders sending them home. It didn't help matters very much that people kept saying helpful things like, "Now, Gayleen, don't get yourself killed on your last shift." As my time got shorter, I became more careful, less reckless than I had ever been. Of course, too much caution can get a person killed too.

The car arrived right on time, carrying with it my three best girlfriends on the force, Karol Chouinard, Carole Coan, and Glenda Lombardo, several bottles of champagne, and a couple of quarts of perfect raspberries. I was *definitely* going to remember that day.

When we got to the Van Nuys station, I asked the driver to pull into the "Official Parking Only" lot, the very one where I had mistakenly put my little car more than twenty years earlier and had gotten into so much trouble. Again I could see people staring out the window, just like before, but this time they were smiling and waving. I waved back. Those years had made an enormous difference in my life. I wasn't shy or nervous or scared of being a cop. I *was* a cop, and I was among friends.

I showed up promptly for 7:15 roll call. People have worn a lot of unlikely getups in roll call, but I believe this was the first time anyone had showed up in a black sequined stripper dress and a police badge. The lieutenant wasn't too thrilled to see the gown, but the guys loved it. When we stood for inspection, they put me right square in the middle, and the lieutenant played it straight. I don't think that even he dared to give me a hard time that morning.

After roll call I said good-bye to all the guys and watched them drive off. I'd known some of them for nearly twenty years. I had one more stop to make before my tour of duty was officially over—an exit interview with Personnel down at Parker Center—but when I saw the cars of my fellow police officers drive out of sight, I knew it was all over.

By the time the limo got us to Parker Center, the news media had heard about the retirement of the LAPD's "last uniformed policewoman," and they all showed up. As I walked out of Parker Center, retirement ID card in hand,

I was interviewed by reporters from newspapers, radio, and television, everyone wanting to know what it was like to be a policewoman and how it felt, after twenty years, to pull the pin. A few inquired about the old Miss Fuzz days. I thought my answers were dazzling—smart, perceptive, very much to the point. Of course, I'd had quite a bit of champagne by then. Looking back on it now, I doubt that I was able to make anyone understand why I was so eager to leave a job I loved so much. Sometimes I wonder myself. Then I remember something my mother used to say: always leave them wanting more. It works for burlesque dancing, and it worked for my life as a cop.

THERE ARE DOZENS of people I've worked with over the years whom I admire, but the only person I ever really idolized was Caroyl, my first training officer, who ran the Van Nuys Jail. I suppose every working woman has a role model, someone who serves as an inspiration early in her career. Caroyl was mine.

On the LAPD training officers are like guardian angels. A cop who is given a new assignment sticks to his training officer like glue for as long as the assignment lasts. They work together, eat together, and take the same days off. I was incredibly lucky in my career, in that I never had a training officer I didn't like. Some of them I liked very much. I *loved* Caroyl.

From the first moment I saw her in action I thought she was everything a policewoman should be, and I wanted to be

just like her. She was built like a nail, short and very, very
skinny. She had a voice unlike anything I had ever heard
before. She could get anyone to do anything she wanted
with that voice. In all the years she'd been in the jail she
never got into a single fight (*altercation*, that is). In fact,
stopping other people's fights with only a few well-chosen
words was her specialty. She used the force of her personality to command, and I found her mesmerizing. I wasn't the
only one who worshipped Caroyl. Most of the policewomen
in the jail fell under her spell too. Many of us went out of
our way to get assigned to her morning watch just so we
could work for her.

Not too long after I joined the force, Caroyl decided to
retire. She had put in her twenty years, she said, and it was
time to call it a day. Everyone was stunned. I was devastated.

"How could she not want to stay on this wonderful job?
She's such a great policewoman. How can she bear to give
it up?" I remember thinking.

In those days I was so excited to be a policewoman that
I could hardly bear to go home at the end of my shift. I
hated days off, and a vacation was unthinkable. I just
wanted to stay in my uniform forever. I wanted Caroyl to
stick around too.

Caroyl didn't say much by way of explanation, just that
she had put in her time and was tired. She was forty-seven
years old, she explained, and she wanted to do something
else with her life besides be a cop. At the time I couldn't
imagine ever feeling the way she did back then. However, a

couple of years ago, when I had put in my twenty years (with my various leaves it took me twenty-two years to do it), I understood her completely. I wasn't burned out or beaten or even discouraged. I was just tired. And at the ripe old age of forty-seven, I too wanted to do something with my life besides be a cop.

The LAPD doesn't take too kindly to early retirement. The department doesn't want cops to stay around forever, mind you, but they prefer it if they put in somewhere between twenty-five and thirty years. They even try to make it worth a cop's while to stay a little longer: after twenty years a cop retires on forty percent salary; with each year up to thirty years that percentage increases. But the incentive plan is apparently not working. More and more cops are doing just what I did and what Caroyl did all those years ago—putting in our twenty and starting a new life as a civilian.

THERE ARE TIMES when I think that my proudest achievement in my twenty years on the police force is that I never made coffee. Well, I almost never made coffee. When I worked the Van Nuys Jail, back in the Dark Ages of the LAPD, policewomen in the women's side of the jail were actually expected to make coffee for the policemen on the other side. Directly after roll call one of the women on duty was supposed to walk over to the men's side and put on a great big pot of coffee.

As soon as I heard about the coffee-making assignment,

I knew there was no way it was going to be included in *this* policewoman's job description. I didn't spend all that time working my ass off in the Police Academy just to be treated like Mrs. Olson. I was determined to buck the system, but not through official protest or even through casual complaints. I decided to do it my way. I fucked it up. It turned out I just wasn't any *good* at making coffee.

First I told everyone that I didn't know how to make it (actually, I'm allergic to it). Then, after four or five people were called in to give me advice, I left such a mess that it took two people to clean it all up. And then, for my *pièce de resistance*, the one time I actually made the stuff, I ended up with thirty-six cups of pure, unadulterated sludge. As if by magic, I was off the coffee detail.

As it happens, I didn't have much of a knack for logging traffic books or filing either, two other chores that were reserved exclusively for policewomen back then. It took me three months to be taken off the traffic book assignment— until the day a supervisor tried to find something and discovered that every piece of paper that had been handled over the previous three months had been either misplaced or misfiled—but I finally did it.

In some ways working in the kit room was the worst "girl's" assignment of all. The kit room officer has the exciting job of dispensing shotgun shells, sending out burglary calls and dispatches, and recharging rovers—those walkie-talkie things that all cops carry. They also have to clean shotguns and check inventory. As you might guess, it was a job reserved strictly for women. (Actually, for "the sick, lame, and lazy" is the way that kind of job was described when I was on the force.) I knew that if I did a halfway decent job of that, all women, including myself, were doomed; I'd never see the light of day again. It didn't go very well right from the start. I lost rovers. I didn't get the shotguns very clean. I never had any idea how many shotgun shells I'd given out. They got me out of the kit room in a hurry.

In all the years I was on the force, that was pretty much my overall approach to any situation that I wanted to change: disappear or use humor rather than confront, and put up a fight only if all else fails. It wasn't my style to make a huge fuss or to come on too strong. I've always believed in being cagy, more political. If a situation called for batting my eyelashes and giggling and acting like a clown, I did it. I was always focused on the end result. After all, the technique worked like a charm when I went undercover and operated pimps and gamblers. Why wouldn't it work on my supervisors? Why shouldn't I use it when I had to work with a difficult partner or a stubborn sergeant? In the end, it got me exactly what I wanted, even if it did give me a reputation as a "character." I didn't mind.

I can't say that too many other female police officers use my approach. My "dizzy blonde" act simply isn't to everyone's taste. I've never seen any point in trying to talk them or anyone else into my point of view. I know I'm not a typical police officer, and I've never wanted to be. If I had been, I never would have survived as long as I did. To me, persuasion and arbitration work a lot better than an "I'm not taking any more of this shit" approach.

There were a lot of changes in my twenty years on the

force, but two stand out far ahead of the pack. One is the use of computers, which has completely revolutionized the way cops do their jobs. The other is the role of women. When I came on the job, women were restricted to Juvenile, Community Relations, the jail, and a few other safe, unexciting spots—no Vice, Homicide, Burglary, Patrol, or Forgery. They couldn't rise above the rank of sergeant. Today all assignments are open to women, and in the LAPD there are six female lieutenants and one female captain. I may even live to see a female police chief.

We have definitely come a long way, baby, but that doesn't mean that sexism, overt and covert, isn't still lingering in the department's ranks. There are still plenty of men around, young guys as well as the old-timers, who think that a policewoman's place is in the kit room counting out shotgun shells. It doesn't matter how good a woman is or how much experience she has on the force; some guys will never think that a woman has any business carrying a badge.

Often I thought that my uniform—at the end, it was the only one with a skirt, remember—was especially galling to some of the men, the ones my friends and I used to call the "male professionals." If I wanted to hold a man's job, how come I didn't wear pants like everyone else? is what their attitudes implied.

God save us all from "male professionalism."

Women do at least as good a job as men. In many areas they're better. Women excel in Juvenile and in Forgery, for example, and they're better equipped to handle cases, such as rapes and child abuse, that require an especially high degree of sensitivity. I think men are better at patrol work, in which the police officer goes out on a call with no idea of what he's walking into. But women officers have a soothing effect; their presence can cool down a hot situation more quickly and easily than the appearance of a man in uniform. Women, just by virtue of being female, are often a calming influence in a crisis.

Although the department didn't generally favor putting women together, I had a lot of women partners over the years, and I always enjoyed the experience, and not just because I didn't have to be bored to death listening to stories about sports or because they usually smelled a lot better. Women are great on the job. I think most female officers really like to work together; no matter what anyone says, we do see our lives and our work differently from the way men see it.

B ACK IN THE spring of 1991, when the LAPD was making headlines all over the world because of that horrible Rodney King video, most of my friends congratulated me on getting off the force while the getting was good. Part of me had to agree with them; it wouldn't have been easy, I'm sure, to walk around the streets of Los Angeles in a police uniform with public sentiment the way it was. Still, relieved as I was not to have to be very involved in the debate, I couldn't help but follow the story with intense interest. I developed strong feelings about what happened and what should be done about it.

I was as shocked to see that video as anyone; I think most cops were. In all my years on the force I never witnessed brutality like that on the job, and I don't know anyone who has (and I do wish I knew exactly what the situation was *before* the video camera started recording). I know that police officers are human, with human weaknesses and frailties and prejudices. They are also different from the rest of the world. Being a cop changes the way you look at things. At everything. Most people look at a street or an apartment house or a bar and see one thing; cops, trained to be suspicious, see something else, often what is going on *behind* the doors. Some cops are jerks. Some cops misuse their authority. Some cops are bigots. (I once worked with a guy who told me that the best orgasm he ever had came when he "shot a nigger in Watts.") But most cops are *none* of those things. They're just hard-working people trying to do the best job they can and trying to get some enjoyment from their lives.

When I joined the force, there were about five thousand cops in the LAPD. Today there are about seven thousand, not much of an increase when you consider how much the crime rate has increased since then. The streets are tough and getting tougher. The police need public support now more than ever. If there are bad cops on the job, LAPD will weed them out. Then we should let the good ones get on with the business at hand.

THE NIGHT BEFORE I retired, as I was choosing the perfect dress to wear for my big day, I went through a lot of the stuff

I've collected over the years. The first thing I came across was that pair of jeans I had from my early days of working hookers, with SWEETCHEEKS written across the backside in rhinestones. I also saw my white fringed sweatshirt and the world's largest collection of tacky wigs. I have my class picture from the Police Academy, the crushed rose from the man I consoled when his daughter was killed, a couple of lamps from the Aloha Room, the house of ill repute my grandmother used to run, and my Miss Fuzz trophy.

I also have, stashed in there with Serina's report cards, hand-painted cards, and God knows what else, twenty years' worth of Performance Evaluation Reports—my years on the force in a nutshell. Twice a year for twenty years my abilities had been rated—reliability, responsiveness, quality of public contacts, thoroughness, initiative, productivity, teamwork, dress, and grooming—and there it all was, laid out in front of me. I thumbed through them quickly, not wanting to get bogged down in too many memories, and saw "Good" and "Excellent" everywhere I looked. I never had a negative report. My eye was caught by one comment I especially liked: "Officer Hays has a good effect on morale."

I loved being a cop. I didn't like the politics or the bullshit, of course, and I'm not crazy about the bad back I've had ever since my days of getting thrown on my tailbone in the Van Nuys Jail or the fact that I seem to be an inch shorter than when I went in. But I miss the people I worked with, and I got satisfaction being able to use what power and authority I had to do people some good. And I *loved* putting bad guys in jail. I'm going to miss that.

One other thing I love, in some ways more than anything

else, is my POLICEWOMAN #1 badge. I fought hard to hold on to it, and it's the last of its kind, a real collector's item. I carried it proudly for twenty years, and when I retired, they let me have it on permanent loan. It symbolizes a lot of what the force was to me and—I hope, given the number one—what I meant to the force. It seems fitting that I should be allowed to keep this piece of official city property. After all, the LAPD will always have a piece of me, too.

ABOUT THE AUTHORS

GAYLEEN HAYS, retired from the Los Angeles Police Department after twenty years, lives in Malibu, California, with her family. Since her retirement she has been writing, acting, and learning how to cross-country ski.

KATHLEEN MOLONEY is the author or coauthor of many books on such diverse subjects as baseball, etiquette, health, business, and ventriloquism. She lives in New York City.